JOB

A STORY OF
UNLIKELY JOY

LISA HARPER

LifeWay Press® Nashville, Tennessee

EDITORIAL TEAM
ADULT MINISTRY PUBLISHING

Faith Whatley
Director, Adult Ministry

Michelle Hicks
Manager, Adult Ministry
Short Term Bible Studies

Mike Wakefield
Content Editor

Sarah Doss
Production Editor

Heather Wetherington
Art Director

Published by LifeWay Press®

© 2018 Lisa Harper
Reprinted July 2018

Lisa Harper is represented by Alive Literary Agency, 7680 Goddard Street, Suite 200, Colorado Springs, CO, 80920. www.aliveliterary.com.

ISBN: 978-1-4627-5127-3

Item: 005795120

Dewey decimal classification: 223.1

Subject headings: JOB, PATRIARCH / BIBLE. O.T. JOB--STUDY AND TEACHING / FAITH

To order additional copies of this resource, write to LifeWay Church Resources Customer Service; One LifeWay Plaza; Nashville, TN 37234; fax 615.251.5933; phone 800.458.2772; email orderentry@lifeway.com; order online at www.lifeway.com; or visit the LifeWay Christian Store serving you.

Printed in the United States of America

Adult Ministry Publishing
LifeWay Church Resources
One LifeWay Plaza
Nashville, TN 37234

CONTENTS

ABOUT LISA

Rarely are the terms "hilarious storyteller" and "theological scholar" used in the same sentence, much less used to describe the same person, but Lisa Harper is anything but stereotypical. She is a master storyteller, whose writing and speaking overflows with colorful pop culture references that connect the dots between the Bible and modern life.

Her vocational resume includes six years as the director of Focus on the Family's national women's ministry, followed by six years as the women's ministry director at a large church. Her academic resume includes a master's in theological studies with honors from Covenant Seminary. Now a sought-after Bible teacher and speaker, Lisa was featured on the national Women of Faith tour and speaks at many other large multi-denominational events—such as Christine Caine's Propel, LifeWay Women events, and Women of Joy conferences—as well as at hundreds of churches all over the world. She's been on numerous syndicated radio and television programs and was featured on the cover of Today's Christian Woman.

Lisa has written more than fifteen Bible studies and books, including *The Sacrament of Happy*, *The Gospel of Mark*, *Believing Jesus*, *Malachi*, *Hebrews*, *Stumbling into Grace*, and *A Perfect Mess*. In spite of her credentials, the most noticeable thing about Lisa Harper is her authenticity. "I'm so grateful for the opportunities God's given me," Lisa says, "but don't forget: He often uses donkeys and rocks!"

INTRODUCTION

Missy and I recently came home from another trip to her home village in Neply, Haiti. (We try to visit a couple of times a year to keep her Haitian roots intact and to share the love of Christ with the community she was born into.) Per usual, the visit prompted several people to ask if it was hard taking her back. My quick and consistent answer: "Yes." Yes, it's very hard to take my precious, healthy daughter back to the place where she almost died—where she was shunned by many villagers when it was revealed that her dear first mama, Marie, died of undiagnosed AIDS and unwittingly infected Missy with HIV, which quickly led to an accompanying tuberculosis infection. It's certainly not easy reestablishing some semblance of real relationship with her extended family members and the caregivers she barely remembers. Nor is it a piece of cake sharing the gospel in an area that's been under the oppressive influence of voodoo for hundreds of years.

Then add in the wilting element of Haiti's weather, which is typically one hundred plus degrees (except for two or three months in the winter when it's still usually at least eighty balmy degrees!), with the humidity levels hovering around the boiling point. Our lodging conditions are usually quite primitive, and both of us inevitably come home to Tennessee with some new skin rash and/or tummy problem. Finally, factor in the reality that every single time we visit her former hometown, we're bombarded by opportunistic people who claim intimacy with Missy—"I'm her first cousin!," "I'm her long-lost uncle!"—in the hopes of exploiting me for money. Frankly, some aspects of our return visits to Haiti aren't just hard—they're messy, emotionally draining, and downright heartbreaking.

But our return visits to Haiti—which, after much wrestling in prayer, I sensed to be an absolute directive from God—are also totally worth it. We've had the pure joy of praying with people there who have committed their lives to Jesus Christ and put their hope in His unconditional love as a direct result of Missy's story. Seeing a child they assumed was dead return thriving and full of joy has been a tangible "show-and-tell" miracle that convinced them of God's redemptive power—of the fact that He really is the Great Physician and Lifegiver. Plus, reconnecting with her biological family has blessed my kid with a beautifully broad and diverse base of familial affection, as well as a precocious awareness of God's sovereign goodness. It speaks to the theologically-foundational and character-forming premise that His providence will never take us to a place where His grace and presence will not envelop and sustain us!

Our Haitian adventures always remind me of something my friend Sheila Walsh often says, "Some of God's greatest gifts to us are wrapped in boxes that cause our hands to bleed when we open them." And it behooves us to have that truism at the forefront of our hearts and minds as we begin this journey through the Book of Job. Because let's admit it—even for most experienced Bible students, the idea of perusing Job sounds about as pleasant as a root canal. Not only does most of Job's story seem to be a painful slog through a swamp of suffering, it also threatens to press on deeply buried bruises left by unanswered questions regarding why God allows suffering and loss in our own lives. Plus, for those brave, wide-eyed ones in your midst who are dipping their toes into group Bible study for the first time—or the first time in a long time—the whole rigmarole of looking up of verses, filling in blanks, and divulging deep thoughts to relative strangers may appear at first to be about as pleasant as sticking their hands in a blender!

So let's make a pact that our journey through Job is going to be a safe place to engage with God, OK? That we're going to be the kind of judgment-free community where every woman feels comfortable asking questions about Him and free enough to share the highs and especially the lows of her personal story. If we do so, I firmly believe the power and authority of God's Word will ultimately guide us to lean more fully into the arms of Jesus, trusting that His presence will be our constant source of joy no matter how difficult or disappointing or even devastating some chapters of our lives may be. In light of that goal, it's not necessary to choose a single group leader for this study. (I can almost hear the audible gasps from the "type As" reading this!) It may actually be more beneficial to choose a couple of friendly chicks to colead, because that will help make the environment less personality-driven and more participation-driven.

HERE ARE A FEW TIPS TO PROMOTE HEALTHY INVOLVEMENT:

- Establish a no-monopoly chat zone. In other words, encourage everyone to answer at least one question rather than having a single windbag, like myself, answer all of them.

- Allow for "silence cushions" between questions to give introverts time to formulate their thoughts and participate.

- Throw spitballs at anyone who responds to a question with a basic yes-or-no answer. (OK, maybe spitballs are a tad punitive, but encourage real responses!)

- Be quick to listen and slow to give advice or attempt to fix the other chicks' problems in your circle. Just say no to Dr. Phil wannabes!

- Make your best effort to begin and end on time.

- Don't focus on moving through all the material each time you get together. Instead, focus on how your small group tribe is marinating in the truths revealed through Job's journey and as a result, leaning into Jesus.

Furthermore, in an effort to make Job more user-friendly, we've created a study guide geared toward participation instead of intimidation. We've segmented it into chunks instead of days so you can complete the questions when you have time—when your baby's sleeping, when your husband's glued to a football game, or when you're finally home from work and have changed into a pair of comfy sweatpants. The last thing we want to do is to make Bible study "homework" so cumbersome and time-consuming that your group dwindles down to nonexistent.

You'll also find a few articles interspersed throughout the study. Hopefully this information from friends and scholars will enhance the study and provide helpful guidance.

We've provided a Leader Helps section in the back of this book to help guide you through the study. It includes a tentative agenda for each session, plus discussion questions to help you debrief each week's personal study. Feel free to adapt it according to your group's size and time constraints.

Doodle wildly in the margins! Be as honest as possible in every response. And feel free to throw this study guide on the floor with a dramatic thwack if something I've written steps on one of your emotional bruises—or hug it close to your chest when Jesus whispers endearments to you through one of the passages or paragraphs on the following pages. My sincere hope and fervent prayer is that the King of all kings will woo us closer to Himself than ever before during this season. That Holy Spirit—our Comforter and Counselor—will seal in us a profound assurance of God's absolute *goodness*—that, much like this Old Testament hero named Job, we'll get to the place of spiritual maturity where we too can earnestly proclaim, "Lord, wherever You lead I will gladly follow. Even if we descend to a valley of suffering where I'm stripped of everything that matters to me and everyone I love, still I will trust in You. As long as You don't take Your presence from me I. Will. Be. OK."

Joyfully Yours,

Lisa

John 16:33 "In this world you will have pain/suffering."

1) Dealing w/ pain - part of our job description.

You can't love well if you can't comfort well.

2) Pain is a great conduit for God's glory.

   * Job was "clean" rich. A good guy doing good things. living a good life.

Satan is not mentioned again after this chapter! But

"I don't deserve this" - is not Biblical.

Pain might be seen as a venue to bring God glory; to honor Job.

* God believes the best of us - Satan? NO

Video sessions available for purchase
or rent at www.LifeWay.com/Job

Job 1:20 = 22

DISCUSSION QUESTIONS:

What one thing from the video teaching was new or interesting to you?

Lisa stated that pain is unavoidable. How has pain touched your life or family?

How is pain a conduit for God's glory?

How have you seen God be glorified through your pain or the pain of someone close to you?

The idea of deservedness is not in the economy of God. But why do we so often live like it is? And how does embracing this non-biblical thought affect our faith?

Have you ever struggled with the reality that really bad things happen to really good people, even the people of God? Explain.

1

SUBTRACTING INSULTS FROM INJURIES

WEEK 1

MY STORY

I wish I could tell you that a profound urge to know how God's presence is always accessible when we're in pain is what compelled me to study Job. But that wasn't it, at least not initially. Nor was this study prompted by a deep longing to connect with Job as an individual. (Frankly some of the physical symptoms he experienced tempt me to scoot my chair away from his because I've never been good with oozing sores and such.) And while I certainly yearn to be more theologically and academically erudite with regard to the entirety of Scripture, I'd be fibbing if I told you that knowledge was my primary motivating factor.

The catalytic incentive that caused me to really delve into this seminal book on human suffering was a homemade version of a Snuggie® Tails™. You know, one of those cheesy, fuzzy blankets that are sewn together at the bottom like a sleeping bag so as to "seal in" the warmth? Yep, a Snuggie. And not a fresh, I-just-ordered-this-from-QVC Snuggie either. But a handmade, grungy, well-worn, prone-to-smell-like-an-active-eight-year-old, oversized sock-blanket that my daughter treasures. She would rather be dragged behind wild horses than sleep without it.

Early one morning, I was standing in front of the stove flipping pancakes. Since we travel quite a bit for work and eat out more often than we should, it's a treat to get to cook in my own kitchen. So I was feeling all content and domestic-goddess-like—with the homemade pancake batter speckled by big, juicy, farm-bought blueberries—and was just about to call for Missy to come downstairs for breakfast when I heard her yelp. The next thing I knew, she was falling head over heels all the way down our long flight of stairs. She slipped on the top tread because she was trying to navigate the steps while wearing that smelly (I've washed it countless times to no avail.), feet-binding blanket. I ran to try to catch my precious baby girl, but before I could get to her, she hit the bottom landing with a sickening thud. My heart echoed a similar thud as I quickly carried my limp child to the couch, praying silently but frantically, "Oh God, please let her be OK! *Please* let her be OK!" Somewhere in the back of my mind this indignant thought stubbornly lodged itself: "I can't believe she's overcome severe malnutrition, cholera, tuberculosis, and HIV only to be seriously injured because of that stupid blanket!"

Missy had knocked the wind out of herself, so it took a few seconds for the bloodcurdling scream to erupt. But when it did, our dog Cookie tucked her tail between her legs and scampered out of the room. Of course, by then I'd already shucked her out of that dreadful tube-of-a-blanket and was running my hands over every inch of her little body feeling for broken bones or serious welts as if desperately trying to read braille from her beautiful, brown limbs. I didn't even realize there were tears running down my face until several minutes later, when Missy's sobs slowed to a whimper and she looked up from the cocoon of my arms and asked, "Did I make you sad, Mama?"

To which this foreign, shrill, put-upon-sounding voice tore from my lungs and bellowed, *Why in the world did you try to walk downstairs in that silly blanket, Honey? You could've really hurt yourself! That scared me to death, Missy. Don't ever, ever wear that blanket when you're going up or down stairs, Baby. Now give me that blanket right now because It. Is. Going. In. The. Trash!*

At which point, my darling miracle of an adopted daughter began to sob again. Good night, I may as well have smacked her in the head for getting a concussion.

> What's one of the worst responses you've had when someone you love got hurt?

Do you tend to run toward people in pain to offer your help, or hope someone else steps in to nurse their wounds? Explain.

Would you rather tend to a physical wound or an emotional wound?

Are you more comfortable offering comfort to someone you love who's suffering or someone you aren't as close to? Explain.

In his profound book *Where Is God When It Hurts?*, Philip Yancey writes: "Pain is a foolproof producer of guilt, I have learned. We all do things we shouldn't … "[1] In other words, when it comes to the waltz of human suffering—whether we're engaged in the dance or simply on the sideline observing—most of us are less than graceful. Sometimes panicked mamas like me berate their precious, post-tumble children. Or, based on the conversation I had with a grieving woman on a flight home from Denver recently, sometimes dear friends deliberately ignore their lifelong besties because they don't know how to respond after the other suffers physical abuse, which leads to a devastating divorce. Or, based on the experience of a friend who lost her teenager in a tragic accident last year, sometimes well-meaning people clumsily attempt to encourage grieving parents by musing out loud that God must've "needed another flower in His garden."

The list goes on and on regarding how our often-abysmal bedside manner adds insult to injury. It's no wonder most people's first choice regarding pain tends to be avoiding it altogether. However, according to Jesus, avoiding pain and hardship in this life is less likely than winning the Powerball®:

> I have told you these things so that in me you may have peace. *You will have suffering in this world.* Be courageous! I have conquered the world.
>
> JOHN 16:33, *EMPHASIS MINE*

Therefore, learning how to better deal with pain and anguish is an absolute necessity.

THE STORY BEHIND JOB'S STORY

One of my favorite *living* theologians (I have platonic crushes on many posthumous dudes including Dr. Charles Spurgeon, Thomas à Kempis, and Andrew Murray.) is Dr. D. A. Carson. He's a seminary professor and author who is often quoted as saying, "A text without a context becomes a pretext for a proof text."[2] In other words, if we don't take the time to consider the culture and climate of the passage we're perusing and how it fits into the whole inscripturated counsel of God, then we'll likely take that passage out of context. We won't understand it or apply it as God purposed. In my experience, when the Word of God is filtered through the minds, pens, and social media accounts of Christ followers, it's *always* distorted at some level. Truthfully, we can't help it because we have finite, human minds. We won't have the perfect mind of God until we're glorified with Him. Therefore, it behooves us to do as much digging as we can into the history and background of whatever scriptural field from which we're hoping to mine redemptive jewels. So grab your pickaxe and one of those mining helmets with the cute light on top, and let's go!

Read 2 Timothy 2:15. Rewrite this New Testament admonition in your own words.

> Be an unashamed worker for God, living according to His Word.

Read Acts 17:10-11. What do you think Paul meant when he described the Bereans as having a "readiness of the mind" (KJV) when it came to the Scriptures?

> they were open to what he said—his message

Who would you describe as being "like a Berean" in your circle of relationships? How does he or she practically demonstrate a passion to know God better through His Word?

Diane → she leans on the word of God to guide her life. She truly prays for any & every decision she must make.

Time Line and Authorship: Job's story seems to take place in the pre-patriarchal/patriarchal era depicted in Genesis. This is evidenced by Job's wealth being determined according to the number of animals he owned and the number of servants he employed (Job 1:3). But the author is unknown, and there's no consensus on the exact date it was written. Jewish rabbinical tradition asserts this book was written in the era of Moses, around 1440 BC. However, others have argued for a Babylonian exile time line—based on the "ongoing suffering" theme of Job—while some modern scholars have argued for dating it much later, well into the Hellenistic period. Therefore, ascribing a composition date for this book is about as imprecise as a game of pin-the-tail-on-the-donkey!

Location: Job's hometown was a place called Uz (Job 1:1), "the precise location of which is unknown. Many modern scholars place it somewhere in the desert south of the Dead Sea, perhaps near Edom (cf. Lam. 4:21; Jer. 25:20). This seems to associate it with Philistine territory or somewhat to the north, in the same vicinity as the homes of Job's three friends (Job 2:11). Others follow Josephus and subsequent Christian and Muslim tradition in placing Uz at Hauron, south of Damascus (possibly the land settled by Aram's son, Gen. 10:23)."[3] I find it interesting that Job was attacked by the "Sabeans" (Job 1:15), who came from Saba in southern Arabia—which is now the country of Yemen—as well as the "Chaldeans" (Job 1:17), who came from Chaldea in southern Mesopotamia—which now includes Iran, Syria, and Turkey. So while we can't pinpoint Job's exact location on GPS, we can safely say his story took place in the Middle East.

Biblical Classification: Rabbis and students of the Hebrew Bible put Job in a small sub-section of books classified as wisdom literature, which includes Proverbs and Ecclesiastes. Their reason for the inclusion of Job is its didactic/instructive content regarding "right living" and/or "right thinking."[4] However, Job indirectly confronts the underlying theme of retribution in Proverbs, which is essentially the idea that *good* *morals lead to a prosperous life, and bad morals lead to folly and destruction.* Which just might be why many contemporary Christian commentarians put the Book of Job in a class by itself, viewing him as more of an individual sport athlete than a team player in the proverbial Olympics of Scripture!

The *Holman Concise Bible Commentary* says it like this:

> Job is in many ways like other writings in the Bible and yet is in a class by itself. Some of the types of biblical material found in Job follow:
>
> **Laments:** Job repeatedly bewailed what had befallen him (Job 3:1-26; 6:2-7; 10:1-12).
>
> **Hymns of Praise:** Job often praised God for His power and righteousness (Job 5:9-16 and 26:5-14).
>
> **Proverbs:** Pithy statements of wisdom and metaphor appear (Job 5:2, 6:5-6, 28:28).
>
> **Prophetic Speech:** The friends sometimes claimed to have had prophetic experiences, and they preached as the prophets did (Job 4:12-14; 11:13-20; 32:8).
>
> **Wisdom Poems:** Job has several lengthy poems on the value of wisdom and right behavior (Job 8:11-22; 28).
>
> **Numeric Sayings:** (Job 5:19)
>
> **Reflective Questioning:** Job sometimes bluntly challenges conventional wisdom (Job 21:17-19).
>
> **Apocalyptic:** Job has some features in common with books like Daniel and Revelation. The earthly struggle is part of a heavenly conflict between God and Satan (Job 1–2). Human foes (Job's wife and three friends) tempt the believer to abandon his perseverance. But faithful endurance leads to triumph and blessings (Job 42).
>
> The Book of Job draws on many types of literature to set forth its message, but it does not belong to any one of these categories. It must be interpreted as unique both in literary type and message. Job is not a conventional book.[5]

Literary Structure: The significant variance of Job's narrative structure (from prose to dialogue) and emotional tone (Job digresses from accepting his fate in the prologue to arguing with God in the middle, speech-oriented section.) has led many Old Testament scholars to surmise that the Book of Job was revised over a period of time.[6] It eventually became a unified literary work, which was ultimately canonized into Holy Writ.

Message and Purpose: Despite the complex theme, unusual literary structure, and some opaque Hebraic terminology, Job is an invaluable book to study and apply to both our everyday lives and theological scaffolding. It's a true story about a real person who was dealt one of the worst hands in history and yet never lost his faith in a good God. This book not only gives us practical advice for how to better deal with pain and suffering, but when read in the context of redemptive history, it's a life-changing literary harbinger pointing us to the perfect sufficiency and salvific miracle found in the cross of Christ! Renowned Australian professor and theologian Dr. Francis Andersen clearly surmises Job's value: "That the Lord himself has embraced and absorbed the undeserved consequences of all evil is the final answer to Job and to all the Jobs of humanity."[7]

What passage or book of the Bible has most consistently and effectively pointed you to the unconditional, sacrificial love of Jesus? How?

John 13
• washing the disciples feet
• new commandment of love

If you were only allowed to read one book of the Bible for the rest of your life, what would it be? Why?

Esther → doing the right thing for the sake of others

JOB'S STORY

As I mentioned in the opening video teaching session, Job's story falls into three clear sections:

Chapters 1–2: A prose prologue that describes earthly and heavenly realms and realities as juxtaposed.[8] A sort of divine competition between good and evil begins with God as the protagonist and Satan as the antagonist.[9]

Chapters 3–42:6: An epic poem—which includes distinct speeches given by Job, his four less-than-helpful friends (Eliphaz, Bildad, Zophar, and Elihu), and ultimately God Himself.[10]

Chapter 42:7-14: A prose epilogue, which depicts Job as a man restored, liberated, at peace, and choosing to be in an obeisant, worshipful relationship with God, his Creator Redeemer.[11]

For a moment, let's explore the last half of the prologue. There we find God, the Creator of the universe, and Satan, the cruel adversary and accuser of humanity, having a second confrontational conversation. The prideful lizard grudgingly acknowledges that Job hasn't yet lost his integrity despite losing his wealth and children. But as we read further, we can almost *hear* the manipulative whine in Satan's tone when he argues that if God would only allow him to afflict Job's flesh and bones, which was previously *not* permitted (1:12), Job's integrity would disappear faster than a mouse at a cat convention!

> One day the sons of God came again to present themselves before the LORD, and Satan also came with them to present himself before the LORD. The LORD asked Satan, "Where have you come from?"
>
> "From roaming through the earth," Satan answered him, "and walking around on it."
>
> Then the LORD said to Satan, "Have you considered my servant Job? No one else on earth is like him, a man of perfect integrity, who fears God and turns away from evil. He still retains his integrity, even though you incited me against him, to destroy him for no good reason."

"Skin for skin!" Satan answered the Lᴏʀᴅ. "A man will give up everything he owns in exchange for his life. But stretch out your hand and strike his flesh and bones, and he will surely curse you to your face."

"Very well," the Lᴏʀᴅ told Satan, "he is in your power; only spare his life." So Satan left the Lᴏʀᴅ's presence and infected Job with terrible boils from the soles of his feet to the top of his head. Then Job took a piece of broken pottery to scrape himself while he sat among the ashes.

JOB 2:1-8

KEY POINTS TO PONDER IN JOB'S STORY

For me, the most difficult concept in Job 2, if not the entire book, is the fact that God *allows* Satan to *further* afflict Job. Good night, the poor fellow has already presided over the funerals of all *ten* of his children and most of his team of employees, plus he's faced foreclosure on his estate. It's almost impossible to imagine the depth of his grief in light of those huge, horrific losses. Now that pain is compounded by adding terribly painful, infected, head-to-toe, open sores to his inventory of agony.

God's sovereignty over absolutely *everything* in the world, including allowing the devil to devastate Job beyond what seems humanly bearable, begs the age-old question we talked about in the first video teaching session: *If God is truly good, why does He allow such bad things to happen to us?* I mean, how in the world could a compassionate Creator hand one of His beloved created beings over to that wicked dragon—the very same snake the apostle John said comes only to steal from us, kill us, and destroy us (John 10:10)? I don't begin to have the wisdom to conclusively answer the question of why God allows suffering. However, over the years, I have constructed an internal theological framework by which to consider God's allowance of suffering so that I don't lose my hope in the ditch of despair, sully my soul in the mud of moralism, trade my peace for the anguish of over-analysis, or harden my heart in the cement of cynicism.

Here's the deal: *Despite how incredibly harsh pain appears from our perspectives, God only gives Satan enough rope to hang himself. It's never enough to drag us away from God's presence.*

At the end of my freshman year in high school, my stepfather gave me a choice; he said if I chose to stay at Lake Brantley High School, I would no longer be allowed to participate in extracurricular activities such as student government, social clubs, or sports. He was the principal at the middle school next door, and he wanted me to ride home with him as soon as he got off work. He was not willing to wait around for me to be finished with track practice or a Fellowship of Christian Athletes meeting. And he flatly refused to drive twenty-five miles round trip after hours to pick me up from anything sports- or social-related.

However, he bargained, if I agreed to transfer to Seminole High School, the secondary school in our town, I could participate in whatever clubs or sports I wanted to because it was close enough for me to ride my bike to and from activities. Mom tried to change his mind after we met with a much less-than-hospitable staff member at Seminole, whose grammar was even more atrocious than his lack of civility. She became concerned about the school's lackluster academic standards, not to mention the rampant drug use, racial tension, and campus violence that was often reported in the local news. Despite the fact that mom graduated from Seminole High School and had met my stepfather, Dad Angel, there thirty years earlier, her concern for my safety and college preparation trumped any nostalgic thoughts of me attending her alma mater.

But Dad Angel wouldn't budge. So in August of 1978, I left all my friends and a sparkling clean, recently built school with a bevy of amenities to attend a very old school with zero modern amenities and a constant police presence. The first few days were definitely dicey. I was chased more than once by a gang leader who wanted to rough me up to bolster his reputation as the number one bully. A girl hurled an expletive at me and threatened to beat me up because her boyfriend gave me directions to the driver's ed class. And my preppy clothes made me a laughingstock at the lockers between classes. But soon enough, I befriended the bully after his sister told him that she and I were friends in elementary school. I learned to avoid boys who were attached to mean, possessive girls who were prone to wearing tube tops in public. And I exchanged khakis and top-siders for Levi's® and flip-flops.

More importantly, I learned to love people who didn't look like me or live in my neighborhood. I learned that skin color, zip codes, and test scores were petty details and absolutely useless qualifiers for real relationships. I learned to make do with hand-me-down uniforms, generously cracked tennis courts, sagging nets, and a gym without air-conditioning in the intense heat and sticky humidity of Central Florida. I learned how to ask better questions in class and check out more books from the library. I learned how to engage through dialogue instead of distancing through diatribe. I learned how to gladly share microscopes and dissecting equipment in an antiquated laboratory under the guidance of an awesome anatomy teacher. I learned how to be a team player and cheer even louder from the bench than I did on the court.

Seminole High School is where I learned that entitlement is the archenemy of creativity, passion, and joy. It's where I learned that building something by the sweat of your brow is a lot more rewarding than having it handed to you. It's where I learned to lead Bible studies with my best friend Cindy. It's where we first studied the theme of adoption in the Bible. It's where we made a solemn promise after a Fellowship of Christian Athletes meeting that we'd adopt hard-to-place kids when we grew up—which means it's also where I unwittingly began the journey of becoming Missy's mama, thirty years before her first mama died from AIDS in a small village in Haiti.

The greatest theological minds in the history of Christendom haven't been able to conclusively answer the question of why our Redeemer allows suffering to happen, so you'd better bet I can't. But I do have enough life experience to believe that if we trust that our God *is good* and He *does good*—even when life is really bad—hardship won't make us bitter; it will actually make us better. It won't break us; it will make us. Of course, changing high schools can only be defined as a "hardship" in the narcissistic milieu of adolescence. It would barely register as a blip on the radar of real pain. But the truism of God's absolute goodness has followed me *all* of my days, including times of much greater grief—my parents' acrimonious divorce, sexual abuse as a child, rape in college, multiple abusive and toxic relationships as a young adult, losing both of my fathers, a heartbreaking failed adoption at the eleventh hour, and many other seasons of suffering.

Now that I'm in my fifties, it's safe to say I've lived more life than I have life left to live. And when I look back over my entire story thus far, I can honestly tell you I have never seen God's back. Mind you, there are still lots of things I don't understand, and there have been losses I almost couldn't bear. But through it all, I have never experienced His absence. I don't know *why* God allows His children to suffer, but I do know that He always makes Himself accessible to us *when* we ache.

Read Psalm 34:18. How would you synopsize this biblical promise into a no-more-than-five-words movie title?

Never Alone ... God is Near.

His wife said to him, "Are you still holding on to your integrity?
Curse God and die!"

"You speak as a foolish woman speaks," he told her.
"Should we accept only good from God and not adversity?"
Throughout all this Job did not sin in what he said.

JOB 2:9-10

What would you guess to be the longest period of time you've ever
gone without "sinning in what you said"?

Egads! A day or 2 maybe

Where do you think your close friends and family members would
rate you on the following scale, with 1 being *slow to speak negative
thoughts and feelings* and 10 being *quick to verbalize your malcontent
and misery?*

Slow to Speak   Quick to Verbalize

1   2   3   (4)   5   6   7   (8)   9   10

friends   *family*

Explain the reason for your score:

*I try not to complain to
friends about pain — my
husband hears about any
& all of them!*

Read Proverbs 10:19. What's the takeaway or application of this verse?

Be slow to speak

I know it's uncool to throw another sister under the bus, but I think it's obvious why Satan didn't kill Job's wife along with his kids—she was more of an asset to the lizard alive than dead! Her nasty comment in Job 2:9, which certainly sounds like she's taunting her own husband to curse God and die, has prompted saints through the ages to vilify her. Saint Augustine called her *diaboli adjutrix* (which in Latin means *devil's advocate*), Saint John Chrysostom labeled her "the devil's best scourge," and John Calvin castigates her as *organum Satani* (which in Latin means *the embodiment of Satan*).[12] But when you consider her excruciating circumstances, it's hard not to agree with pastor and author Stuart Briscoe (whose wife Jill is one of the wisest, loveliest, and most humble Bible teachers I've ever had the privilege of listening to) who charitably insists, "She deserves a fairer judgment."[13]

To be fair, Mrs. Job had more than enough reasons to rail against God. Those seven sons and three daughters were her children too. Her grief was surely at least as deep as Job's. Her mother's heart had been shattered into a million, jagged pieces, which had sheared off her joy and every bit of faith she had in the goodness of Yahweh. Prior to her outburst, she was likely still in a state of shock, trudging in a slow circle around town like a zombie. Then perhaps one day—not long after the day of disaster—while making her sad loop, she looked up to see her husband sprawled on top of the town trash dump in the smoldering ashes of everyone's discarded newspapers and coffee grinds, covered with oozing, infected ulcers. It probably took a minute for her foggy mind to comprehend the scene she had stumbled upon. But when the picture finally came into focus, she realized he was scraping himself with the edge of a plate she'd thrown against the kitchen wall of their tiny rental house in despair. At that point, Mrs. Job just flat lost it.

If we're being honest, I bet most of us can identify with her. My sweet daughter could actually give you recent times and dates when I've channeled a little Lady Job. In fact, just this week I was so physically and emotionally depleted from working and traveling way too much while battling the flu, that when she mildly misbehaved, I bellowed, "*Melissa, I* have had *it! I will not tolerate this kind of disobedience anymore!"* To say I overreacted would be putting my bad behavior mildly. So yeah, I can absolutely understand Mrs. Job's ugly retort. I'm not saying it's OK or innocuous—especially the cussing God part—but given her very bad, horrible, no good string of days, the eruption makes total sense. And I think Job had grace for her heretical fury too. Unlike ancient church fathers, he didn't call her the devil's personal assistant or a wicked hussy. He simply said she was being foolish. And who knows but what he pulled her into his bleeding arms when he said it, because he of all people knew the raw grief that incited her rage. Then he articulated the most brilliant, sound theological position one could ever assume in the midst of suffering: *"Should we accept only good from God and not adversity?"*

And that, ladies and gentleman, is called serving dessert first, because learning to accept everything that sifts through the sovereignty of God's hands is the main takeaway of Job! It is truly the crux of this story and the unquenchable pilot light of personal joy.

YOUR STORY

What's the most painful thing you experienced as a child?

Growing up w/ an alcoholic father & seeing what it did to my mother.

What's the most painful thing you experienced as an adolescent or young adult?

I was pretty miserable when I went away to college.

What's the most painful thing you've experienced recently?

Watching friends deteriorate mentally & physically

How do you think those experiences have shaped or altered your view of God?

I lean more on God for grace, understanding, patience & positive outlook God is good... all the time!

In C. S. Lewis's classic book, *The Lion, the Witch, and the Wardrobe*, there's a wonderful scene in which Mr. Beaver is talking about Aslan the Lion (the Christ figure in this awesome allegorical tale) with Susan, a young girl. Their conversation goes like this: "'Aslan is a lion—*the* Lion, the great Lion.' 'Ooh!' said Susan. 'I'd thought he was a man. Is he—quite safe? I shall feel rather nervous about meeting a lion.' ... 'Safe?' said Mr. Beaver ... 'Who said anything about safe? 'Course he isn't safe. But he's good. He's the King, I tell you.'"[14]

How do you reconcile the idea that our Savior isn't safe but He's good with the psalmist's declaration that God is his safe refuge in Psalm 91:2?

Bad things are still going to happen in this world but God will always be our good Father, to walk w/ us through all the bad.

If you could fashion God to be either only safe or only good, which would you choose? Explain.

Good - I need him more that way.

Do you feel like the pain you've experienced in life has put distance between you and God or prompted you to lean into Him more fully?

Read Psalm 139:23-24. Spend a few moments prayerfully meditating on these verses, and then list any way you may have offended or grieved God (v. 24) in how you've handled hardship.

Anger
Selfishness
Jealousy

In light of that passage, has the Holy Spirit convicted you of any patterns, habits, or behaviors that need to change regarding how you might react to hardship in the future? If so, what changes are you committed to make?

Look at my blessings first instead of desiring what others have or can do.
Stay away from pity parties.
Acknowledge how good the Lord has been & will continue to be in my life.

THE MESSAGE AND PURPOSE OF JOB

BY E. RAY CLENDENEN

What do we mean when we say we are looking for the message and purpose of the Book of Job? Are we asking, "What did Job learn from his experience?" If so, then the answer would have to come from God's speeches in Job 38–41, and it would deal with the greatness of God's wisdom and power. But Job never knew the rest of the story; he never knew about the conversation between God and Satan in the prologue. The story of Job is bigger than the story of Job's experience. The message and purpose of the Book of Job must include the whole book: the prologue, dialogues, and epilogue. The message and purpose are more than what Job learned, although that must be included.

EXPLANATIONS

Chrysostom (ca. AD 347-407), relying solely on the prologue, "found in Job a model of self-denial for those struggling with the devil, and his perseverance under trial was therefore to be imitated."[15] On the other hand, Jerome (ca. AD 347-419) saw the book's message in Job's testimonies to his faith in the coming Redeemer and in the resurrection (19:25-27).[16]

A common view is that the purpose behind the story of Job is to refute the principle of retribution in this life, which is clearly a dogma Job's companions held. The retribution principle claims that righteousness always brings prosperity and happiness, whereas wickedness brings misery. Even Job himself believed (as many do today) that the innocent should not experience great suffering; this should rather be reserved for the wicked who thumb their noses at God. The book certainly overturns this dogma. But is this the primary message?

This view does not seem to do justice to all the parts of the book—for example, God's speeches in Job 38–41.

Another potential purpose for the book is to resolve the problem of suffering or of innocent suffering. Job did wrestle with this issue and asked about it, but he never received an answer. The answer the reader gains from the prologue surely applies only in Job's case. The book does not answer the problem of suffering.

Another explanation about the book's message and purpose is that the story shows that God will show up in the midst of suffering and comfort the sufferer. "[T]hough men must suffer in the dark, their very suffering may be an enrichment if in it they know the presence of God, who is ever ready to dwell with him who is of a crushed ... and humble spirit."[17] Although true in some sense, this is not the book's message. Sufferers cannot expect a revelation of God like Job received. God's revelation did not bring Job comfort; it caused him to repent. Besides, this solution fails to take into account the prologue and epilogue.

LESSONS

What may we learn from the Book of Job if we consider all its parts? First, we observe in the prologue that God is the One who points the finger at Job because he clearly delights in the Lord. Three times the prologue states Job was a man of integrity (1:1,8; 2:3, HCSB). The Hebrew word translated "integrity" (yashar) can refer to something straight or level or that conforms to a standard. When speaking of a person, yashar often translates into English as "upright" and refers to someone (1) whose way of life conforms to what is right and (2) who follows the Lord's ways, His ethical and moral standards of behavior. Three times the story says Job feared God and turned away from evil (1:1,8; 2:3). One who fears God seeks to live in accordance with His will, and thus to turn away from behavior that would be contrary to that will.

But Satan raised an important issue. Why did Job behave uprightly? Was it so God would bless him with material prosperity, a large family, and good health? Or did Job live with integrity because he delighted in the Lord and His ways? With Job, Satan was just following what he had done as the serpent in the garden—questioning God's character and trying to ruin His worshipers.[18] According to the prologue in Job, Satan failed this time. Job responded, "Should we accept only good from God and not adversity?" And the narrator adds that "throughout all this Job did not sin in what he said" (2:10; see 42:7-9, HCSB).

Second, we observe in the dialogue the rest of the story, but this is much messier. John Walton, an Old Testament scholar, has observed that throughout Job's dialogue with his four companions, three claims were on the table: the retribution principle (Job was being punished for sin), Job's righteousness, and God's justice.[19] Representing ancient pagan wisdom, Eliphaz, Bildad, and Zophar advocated the retribution principle, accepted God's justice, but rejected Job's righteousness. Job advocated his righteousness, accepted the retribution principle, and rejected God's justice. Representing Israelite wisdom, Elihu (who had a Hebrew name) advocated God's justice, accepted the retribution principle, but rejected Job's claims of righteousness as arrogance. Suffering, Elihu claimed, had a disciplinary and preventative purpose.

Job's first three companions wanted him to manipulate God by a tactic of appeasement: Job should confess to a long list of sins until he came to the one (or more) that had gotten him into such trouble. Then God would have to forgive Job and bless him again. Job, being a man of integrity, refused to confess to sins he had not committed. He considered his innocence more important than restored blessings (27:1-6). Furthermore, Job reminisced about his former life and showed that what he missed most was not his material blessings but the opportunity to pursue righteousness in the public square (ch. 29). Clearly Satan's charge that Job served God in return for blessings was false.[20] Furthermore, as harsh as Job's cries of injustice were at times (e.g., 9:21-24; 10:13-17; 12:13-25), he continued to cry out in his pain to God. He never turned his back on God, but continued to pursue Him, considering God his only hope.[21] (See 13:22-24; 16:19-21; 19:27; 31:35-37.)

When God spoke (chaps. 38–41), He neither defended Himself against Job's charges nor explained Job's suffering. To do so would mean that faith must be based on understanding rather than on knowing the God who created all things and maintains order in the cosmos. God demonstrated to Job that He is worthy of man's delighting in Him. Job thus laid aside all of his earlier claims and submitted in faith to the God who rules with wisdom, power, and grace. God demonstrated His grace by restoring prosperity to His servant in whom He took delight. And Job came to know God better than he ever had before. He is "the Rock— His work is perfect; all His ways are entirely just. A faithful God, without prejudice, He is righteous and true" (Deut. 32:4, HCSB).

Adapted from E. Ray Clendenen, "The Message and Purpose of the Book of Job," *Biblical Illustrator*, Summer 2013, 22-25.

Job 3: 24-26 ; 1 King 19: 1-7 Elijah Flees

God accomodates human frailty.

God encourages us to come to him w/ all our emotions.

Don't deny God! Don't give up.

Get mad but don't lose hope in God.

God does not practice reciprocity —

Grief is a sign of hope

Job 3 is example → his grief → hope

Grief → the hope that God will rescue us

Video sessions available for purchase
or rent at www.LifeWay.com/Job

DISCUSSION QUESTIONS:

What one thing from the video teaching was new or interesting to you?

When have you struggled to be totally honest with God—to express your deepest emotions to Him?

What did Lisa mean when she said, "It's not the way we grieve that distances us from God, it's what we grieve." Have you ever found yourself grieving the "wrong" thing? Explain.

Why does honesty about pain and suffering drive some people away? When was a time this happened to you?

Why is the prevailing thought that if something bad is happening to me, I must have done something bad to deserve it? Have you ever struggled with this thought? Explain.

How is grief a sign of hope?

2

THE LONELY
AISLES·
OF ACHE

READING ASSIGNMENT:

Peruse Job 3–11 between now and watching the next video teaching. Feel free to read it in sections (maybe one chapter at a time). If possible, try to read through all nine chapters at least twice so that the meaning behind these words begins to sink in.

MY STORY

Soon after my parents divorced, Dad remarried and moved out of the city to forty-two acres of flat, cactus-dotted pastureland in central Florida. He went there to begin his dream of becoming a cattleman-rancher. Before the moving boxes were all unpacked, Dad took me to the feed store to pick out my very first saddle—a beautiful, hand-tooled leather model with fancy, silver concha decorations. I was so proud of that saddle and even more proud when the store owner winked at Dad and asked, "Is this your new ranch hand, Everett?" And Dad said, "Yep, she sure is!" Then, when he put his big hand on my little girl shoulder as we were walking out to the truck and said he was really going to need my help with our new cattle operation, I stretched at least an inch or two taller!

I'm sure I was more nuisance than asset those first few years of working cows with Dad. I wasn't big enough to hold them still for vaccinations and wasn't yet strong enough to circle a rope over my shoulder and lasso a calf while riding my beloved horse, Gypsy, even though I practiced roping fence posts by the barn every single weekend I got to be with Dad. Despite my ineptitude, I fell madly in love with taking care of our farm animals. The menagerie included five horses, fifty or so dairy cows that Dad fussed over, twenty or so pigs he kept mostly for meat, a motley crew of hens who insisted on laying eggs in the horse troughs instead of their nests, a couple of precious mutts, and even our mean old rooster who angrily chased my stepbrother and me on a regular basis.

One summer, one of our mama cows died before weaning her calf. While I was sad to see the mama go, I was thrilled when Dad asked me to nurse her calf with a bottle until it got strong enough to fend for itself. I named the solid black, orphaned calf Inky and spent every waking moment tending to him. It wasn't long before he bonded to me, no longer staying in the pasture with the rest of the herd but instead following me around like an oversized puppy. He even started sleeping outside the house, curled up in the wobbly circle of our snoring dogs. They completely accepted Inky despite the fact that he mooed instead of barked.

When my sweet baby bull was about a year old, Dad told me it was time to assimilate him back into the herd. I cried, insisting that Inky didn't know how to be a cow anymore because he'd become part of our family. But when Dad gently encouraged me that we had to do what was best for Inky, I relented, knowing deep in my heart that Inky needed to be with his *real* family. When I was at Dad's, I still made several visits to the fence every day to rub Inky's growing black head and feed him treats. Not too long after we transitioned him from pet back to farm animal, a pack of rabid dogs attacked and killed several of our newborn calves, including Inky. Dad teared up when he gave me the news. He explained sorrowfully that even though Inky was a yearling and big enough to defend himself, he probably didn't because he thought of dogs as friends not as potentially dangerous enemies.

I was crushed. My less-than-tender stepmother drove me down to the pasture while Dad was on the tractor trying to bury the corpses. When I saw Inky's remains, I was inconsolable. I sobbed and sobbed, devastated by the realization that had I not turned Inky into a pet, he never would've been savagely attacked and killed. I couldn't help imagining him trotting over to that pack of wild dogs with his bright eyes and friendly disposition, assuming they wanted to play with him like our other dogs always did.

When Dad came up from the barn to clean up, my stepmother announced in an irritated huff that she was leaving to go shopping in town because she was sick of hearing me cry and carry on over a stupid cow. That mini-tragedy took place when I was eleven years old. It was the first time (although certainly not the last) it occurred to me that grief is not an inclusive kind of emotion. That deep ache tends to be an isolating event. That despair tends to put uncomfortable distance between the heartbroken and the observers. Especially if the observers haven't healthily processed their own grief and loss.

As American poet Ella Wheeler Wilcox observed in her most enduring work, *Solitude*:

Laugh, and the world laughs with you;
  Weep, and you weep alone,
For the sad old earth must borrow its mirth,
  But has trouble enough of its own.
Sing, and the hills will answer;
  Sigh, it is lost on the air,
The echoes bound to a joyful sound,
  But shrink from voicing care.

Rejoice, and men will seek you;
  Grieve, and they turn and go.
They want full measure of all your pleasure,
  But they do not need your woe.
Be glad, and your friends are many;
  Be sad, and you lose them all—
There are none to decline your nectar'd wine,
  But alone you must drink your gall.

Feast, and your halls are crowded
  Fast, and the world goes by.
Succeed and give, and it helps you live,
  But no man can help you die.
There is room in the halls of pleasure
  For a large and lordly train,
But one by one we must all file on
  Through the narrow aisles of pain.[1]

Would you describe the most painful season of your life as a lonely time? Why or why not?

Lonely → did not lean on God @ that time. No one understood my pain.

Are you more comfortable crying alone or crying on a friend or loved one's shoulder? Explain.

Usually, I need to be held & comforted.

When was the last time you cried alone or on someone's shoulder? Why were you upset?

The last time was when I hit bottom & sunk into depression. I cried sorrowful tears on Bob's shoulders.

Read 1 Samuel 20:41. Would your close friends and family members describe you as someone who weeps "more," like David? Or would they describe you as a stoic who doesn't cry very easily?

Weep like David!

JOB'S STORY

We'd be hard pressed to find anyone else in human history who walked "the narrow aisles of pain"[2] more solitarily than Job did. Before the prologue of his story was even finished he'd lost almost everyone who really mattered to him—except for his wife, who's more salt-in-his-wounds than comfort at this point, and a few so-called friends. They, much like my stepmother, quickly revealed their distaste for Job's honest despair, distancing themselves from the awkward messiness of his grief with condescending admonitions veiled in flowery poetry. Eliphaz said:

> A word was brought to me in secret;
> my ears caught a whisper of it.
> Among unsettling thoughts from visions in the night,
> when deep sleep comes over men,
> fear and trembling came over me
> and made all my bones shake.
> I felt a draft on my face,
> and the hair on my body stood up.
> A figure stood there,
> but I could not recognize its appearance;
> a form loomed before my eyes.
> I heard a whispering voice:
> "Can a mortal be righteous before God?
> Can a man be more pure than his Maker?"
> If God puts no trust in his servants
> and he charges his angels with foolishness,
> how much more those who dwell in clay houses,
> whose foundation is in the dust,
> who are crushed like a moth!
> They are smashed to pieces from dawn to dusk;
> they perish forever while no one notices.
> Are their tent cords not pulled up?
> They die without wisdom.
> *Call out! Will anyone answer you?*
> *Which of the holy ones will you turn to?*

JOB 4:12–5:1, *EMPHASIS MINE*

In other words, *Job, you obviously have hidden sin in your life, which is the reason you're in this pit of destruction. So you may as well quit whining because no one's even listening to your prayers.*

In chapter 8, Bildad weighed in:

> How long will you go on saying these things?
> Your words are a blast of wind.
> Does God pervert justice?
> Does the Almighty pervert what is right?
> Since your children sinned against him,
> he gave them over to their rebellion.
> But if you earnestly seek God
> and ask the Almighty for mercy,
> if you are pure and upright,
> then he will move even now on your behalf
> and restore the home where your righteousness dwells.
> Then, even if your beginnings were modest,
> your final days will be full of prosperity.
>
> For ask the previous generation,
> and pay attention to what their fathers discovered,
> since we were born only yesterday and know nothing.
> Our days on earth are but a shadow.
> Will they not teach you and tell you
> and speak from their understanding?
> Does papyrus grow where there is no marsh?
> Do reeds flourish without water?
> While still uncut shoots,
> they would dry up quicker than any other plant.
> Such is the destiny of all who forget God;
> the hope of the godless will perish.

JOB 8:2-13

In other words, *Job, you're a big, fat, guilty windbag, and your children deserved to die.*

Zophar then piled on in chapter 11:

> Should this abundance of words go unanswered
> and such a talker be acquitted?
> Should your babbling put others to silence,
> so that you can keep on ridiculing
> with no one to humiliate you?
> You have said, "My teaching is sound,
> and I am pure in your sight."
> But if only God would speak
> and open his lips against you!
> He would show you the secrets of wisdom,
> for true wisdom has two sides.
> Know then that God has chosen to overlook some of your iniquity.

JOB 11:2-6

In other words, *Job, I wish you'd shut up because you're getting on my last nerve, and if God wasn't God, He'd be sick of you too.*

When my stepmother callously referred to Inky as a "stupid cow," she was technically correct. Bovine creatures don't come close to the intellectual capacity of humans. However, she's the one with a lower-than-average emotional IQ because of her inability to recognize that legitimate affection—therefore real relationship—can exist between beasts and men. She was oblivious to the fact that I had a real bond with that baby bull, which is why she could so easily dismiss my grief as adolescent drama.

That's essentially the chasm that becomes apparent between Job and these three miserable comforters. Everything they say to Job isn't technically wrong. Frankly, most of what they say about God's inscrutability is accurate. They're right on target when they describe His divine supremacy. But the spirit of what Eliphaz, Bildad, and Zophar preach is crooked because they're oblivious to the fact that Job has a relationship with his Creator. Therefore, while his grievances against God may have rung audaciously in their hypocritical ears, Job still had a right to air them because of the very real bond that existed between him and his heavenly Father.

Is it OK to question God? What do you surmise from reading the following passages:

Psalm 10

Habakkuk 1:1-11

They all ask plenty of questions

Mark 15:33-34 *"My Lord, my Lord - why have you forsaken me..."*

Luke 1:26-38

But now read:

1 Samuel 28:1-6 *Lord did not answer Saul*

Luke 1:5-20 *Zechariah was muted for his unbelief.*

What's the <u>difference</u>?

Saul & Zechariah wanted proof -
The first set questioned why, where...

Questions that come from desperation, confusion, and sincere wonder are welcomed by the Lord. We have the freedom to bring these before God. However, questions born out of disobedience, skepticism, and disbelief are not met with the same response. Questioning God about timing and purpose is one thing, but questioning His character is another.

Read Hebrews 11:6. What hint does this verse give regarding how to approach God when we have doubts or questions? What would it look like to apply this verse practically the next time you aren't thrilled about where God's directing your path?

Without faith it is impossible to please God; if you draw near to God - you must believe that He exists.

KEY POINTS TO PONDER IN JOB'S STORY

One of my favorite lecture series in seminary was about having a "high view" of God. I dug through my old notes from that series and discovered that our professor taught from Isaiah 6 as his main text.

> In the year that King Uzziah died, I saw the Lord seated on a high and lofty throne, and the hem of his robe filled the temple. Seraphim were standing above him; they each had six wings: with two they covered their faces, with two they covered their feet, and with two they flew. And one called to another:
>
> Holy, holy, holy is the Lord of Armies;
> his glory fills the whole earth.
>
> The foundations of the doorways shook at the sound of their voices, and the temple was filled with smoke.
>
> Then I said:
>
> Woe is me for I am ruined
> because I am a man of unclean lips
> and live among a people of unclean lips,
> and because my eyes have seen the King,
> the Lord of Armies.
>
> Then one of the seraphim flew to me, and in his hand was a glowing coal that he had taken from the altar with tongs. He touched my mouth with it and said:
>
> Now that this has touched your lips,
> your iniquity is removed
> and your sin is atoned for.
>
> Then I heard the voice of the Lord asking:
>
> Who should I send?
> Who will go for us?

I said:

Here I am. Send me.

And he replied:

Go! Say to these people:
Keep listening, but do not understand;
keep looking, but do not perceive.
Make the minds of these people dull;
deafen their ears and blind their eyes;
otherwise they might see with their eyes
and hear with their ears,
understand with their minds,
turn back, and be healed.

Then I said, "Until when, Lord?" And he replied:

Until cities lie in ruins without inhabitants,
houses are without people,
the land is ruined and desolate,
and the LORD drives the people far away,
leaving great emptiness in the land.
Though a tenth will remain in the land,
it will be burned again.
Like the terebinth or the oak
that leaves a stump when felled,
the holy seed is the stump.

ISAIAH 6:1-13

I remembered the lively discussions we had in class regarding how in modern Christendom's quest to make the gospel relevant to teenagers and unbelievers we've all but lost the kind of awed reverence Isaiah displayed toward God. Our bumper-sticker-theology, God-is-my-copilot kind of culture has unwittingly minimized the omniscience, omnipotence, and perfect righteousness of the Alpha and Omega. We've sacrificed His greatness in our attempt to make Him more accessible. I remember being convicted during that class that I didn't revere God the way I should. At that point, I committed to be more circumspect in how I addressed Him in prayer and even how I carried His Word. I chose to regard my Bible as a precious treasure instead of carelessly shoving it into a suitcase or tossing into the back seat of the car on a road trip. I still hold to those convictions.

However, as I look back over my walk of faith in the twenty years since seminary, it's clear that I sometimes overcorrected and ended up in the opposite ditch—having too low of a view of myself. I began to teach Bible studies about "awe deprivation," focusing on the danger of having an anemic view of God. I loved to quote the Latin phrase, *mysterium tremendum* (tremendous mystery), which I gleaned from my one of my faith heroes, A. W. Tozer.[3] I also began weaving the word *depravity* into sober conversations as often as I could when describing how I was saved purely by grace from a sinful pit I'd dug myself and how I deserved death because of my transgressions. It all sounded really lofty and academic to me at the time because I didn't have the spiritual maturity to understand that having a truly high view of God doesn't result in continuing to have a low, degrading opinion of ourselves post-conversion. Instead, having a high view of God opens the believer's heart and mind to what God says about us, His beloved children. Yes, apart from Him we're wicked and depraved, but after we put our faith and hope in Jesus Christ, we're allowed to shrug into His robes of righteousness and are adopted into the family of God as full heirs!

(handwritten margin note: high view of God should result in high view of self)

Where would you put yourself on the *View of God* scale?

Low   High
1   2   3   4   5   6   7   8   9   (10)

Where would you put yourself on the *View of Self* scale?

Low   High
1   2   3   4   5   6   7   (8)   9   10

If we give Job's three friends a big benefit of the doubt, we can assume they had mostly good intentions when they delivered their self-righteous lectures. However, like a young seminarian armed with more head knowledge than spiritual maturity, their arrows missed the mark by a country mile! Just look at the difference between Bildad's last recorded description of mankind and the apostle Paul's description of us:

> If even the moon does not shine
> and the stars are not pure in his sight,
> how much less a human, who is a maggot,
> a son of man, who is a worm!
> JOB 25:5-6

For we are his workmanship, created in Christ Jesus for good works, which God prepared ahead of time for us to do.

EPHESIANS 2:10

God is great and you are a worm may sound all humble and pious initially, but the "woe is you" part still puts the emphasis squarely on the frailty of man instead of the faithfulness of God. It may appear to be the opposite of arrogance, but it's actually just narcissism in a nicer outfit—because it's still all about us. Genuine Christian humility shifts the focus from our innate worminess to our Redeemer's amazing grace, which has the power to transform creepy crawlers into beautiful butterflies! We'll never experience wide-eyed spiritual awe while camping out in the dry land of our own deficiency. Open-mouthed wonder that morphs into belly-laughing gratitude only happens when we pick up our tents and move into the glorious land of God's miraculous sufficiency!

KEY CHARACTER IN JOB'S STORY

Although I loathe giving that lying lizard, Satan, any more ink in this Bible study—especially since we've already established that contrary to popular assumption he's only a bit player in this story and isn't mentioned again after Job 2—he is the merchant who compiled, marketed, and sold the shame that Eliphaz, Bildad, and Zophar are dumping on Job by the wheelbarrow load. Frankly, I think Satan is always the supplier of shame. He doesn't have the ability to create like God does, and shame is not a created substance. It is instead the amalgamation of lies, wounds, offenses, abuse, and fear that make up the detritus of our lives, which that dirty dragon gathers gleefully while slithering—hidden and unbidden—through the dark alleys of our personal history. Then he boils all those ugly memories and painful chapters of our stories into a toxic brew that we often swallow because it smells vaguely familiar.

For instance, when that woman from church told me I wasn't a good candidate for motherhood because I'd been sexually abused as a child and raped as a young woman and might unwittingly transfer some of the trauma I'd experienced onto a child of my own, it sounded plausible. Her indictment echoed my greatest, albeit mostly subconscious, fears. I worried, *What if I didn't process everything I needed to in therapy? What if that awful stain from my past could soil my future? What if my parenting would somehow make some precious, innocent little punkin' more predisposed to sexual abuse?*

When I consider the seven years I could've been in the fostering or adoption process but was instead trapped in an ugly, Satan-authored, perversion of the truth, it's all I can do not to shake my dear, still shame-bound friends by the shoulders and bellow, *Quit listening to the lizard!* That scaly liar will always hiss lies that distance us from God. But if we listen wisely, then we'll realize Satan typically overplays his hand, inciting unnecessary drama instead of alleviating real trauma. His version of truth is like an IED (improvised explosive device). It's devised to maim, kill, and inflict as much damage as possible. God's truth is more like a surgeon's scalpel, meant to excise damaged tissue with minimal invasion so we can heal quickly and go on to live healthier, more abundant lives.

We're going to explore the issue of shame versus repentance later on in this study because it comes up again toward the end of Job's journey. For now, let's begin inventorying the shame bombs the lizard has hatefully lobbed into the vulnerable parts of our hearts and minds.

What recycled lie or wound from your past has Satan used most often in an attempt to ensnare you in shame? What truth has God given you to combat that lie? What keeps you from consistently applying that truth?

not worthy because of
dads alcoholism
I am a child of God - a princess
to the King ; fearfully & wonderfully
made

Read 1 Corinthians 6:1-8. What difference do you see between the accountability that Paul calls the church to in this passage and being bound by Satan-authored shame?

We should be above the law -
suffer the wrong, suffer the
defeat > don't wrong & defraud
your brothers

Read 1 Peter 5:8-9. How would you paraphrase this passage in a way a child could understand it?

Don't allow Satan to
tell you lies! Stand
firm in your faith -
God will always love you.

Read Ephesians 6:11-17 How does putting on the armor of God help you battle the enemy in his desire to heap shame on you?

Knowing what the Bible
says, gives us the truth
to fight off the devil -

Soon after I brought Missy home from Haiti I taught her the saying, "Harper girls do trauma not drama." I explained that if her heart or her body were hurt then she should cry as loud and as long as she needed to and I would take care of her. But I told her, if she cried and carried on about something that wasn't serious or wounding—such as wanting to play another game on the iPad® or wanting a Fruit Roll-Up™ even though she hadn't eaten her dinner yet—that was called drama. Between the amped up sensation of reality television, the shrieking discord of current political affairs, and the twenty-four/seven barrage of social media, I think our culture is so saturated with drama that too often real trauma goes unnoticed and untended. We rush to triage emotional hangnails but completely ignore people around us who are bleeding out.

Poor Job was essentially lying with his chest open on the operating table, and his friends were too busy proclaiming theatrical, spiritually-varnished platitudes to even hand him a roll of gauze.

Evangelist, preacher, and author Dwight L. Moody (who founded the Moody Bible Institute in Chicago) once said, "We have been preaching too much and sympathizing too little."[4]

With regard to your circle of Christian friends, would you say this is at least partly true? Explain.

NO - there is a great deal of sympathy & prayers for others in whatever difficulties they face.

Have you ever had a friend comfort you well by just *being there* for you (like Mr. Ed from Eva's story in our teaching video)? Why do you think presence is often more comforting than conversation when we're in acute pain?

you are often not in a place to even hear the words. you just want to be held & feel the comfort of another.

Read Psalm 139 slowly. Now reread it, but insert your name everywhere there's a personal pronoun, such as "I." Print or write this psalm, and place it somewhere you'll see it often. Tape it to your bathroom mirror, refrigerator, or car dashboard. Commit to reading it out loud every single day for a month so as to firmly establish or re-establish your identity in Christ.

GROUP ACTIVITY (OPTIONAL)

Go to a home improvement store, a gardening store, or a landscaping company/nursery, and get light-colored river rocks that are three to four inches in diameter. You'll need one for each person in your group. Take ample time to think about the biggest/hardest question you have for God, and then write that question on your personal rock with a black marker.

At an appointed time, gather together with your *Job* Bible study friends at a lake, pond, creek, reservoir, or river, and, one at a time, toss your stones into the water. Finish with a time of prayer after all the rocks have been thrown. Realize that some may want to relinquish their "rights" to have their questions answered. Some may want to express their confusion or anger at God's inscrutability, while others may simply want to reaffirm their trust in God's sovereignty despite the fact that they still have unanswered questions. Once everyone has expressed their feelings honestly—without any judgment or commentary from the rest of the group—carpool to the nearest Mexican restaurant and thoroughly enjoy copious bowls of tortilla chips dunked in vats of hot queso as well as mounds of fresh, tableside guacamole!

JOB'S FRIENDS: MODELS OF COMPASSION?

BY J. MARK TERRY

All of us have gone to visit a grieving friend and have wondered what to say. Sometimes we say nothing. Other times when we do talk, we later question whether we said the right thing. Many times we hear what others say, and we are sure they said the wrong thing. Job's friends came to see him as he grieved over the deaths of his children (Job 2:11). How effectively did they comfort their friend? A careful study of Job's three friends and their efforts will help us all become better comforters.

The Bible tells us Eliphaz, Bildad, and Zophar learned of Job's despair and agreed to meet and travel together to visit Job (v. 11). This demonstrates they knew each other and Job before the sad events transpired. Evidently, they all were old and good friends. The three came to visit Job, mourn with him, and comfort him. Clearly, sincere concern prompted their visit, and they meant for their words to console Job in his loss and instruct him in righteousness.[5]

When the three friends approached Job, they barely recognized him at all. Suffering and illness had altered his appearance. Grief overcame them, and they dramatically expressed their anguish. First, they wept loudly for their friend and his suffering. Second, they tore their robes. Third, they sprinkled dust on their heads. All of these actions expressed deep sorrow. Beyond these actions, they sat silently in Job's presence for seven days and seven nights. This period of mourning was typical of mourning for a prominent person (Gen. 50:10). It showed their respect for Job and their identification with his sorrow.[6] Who were these concerned friends?

ELIPHAZ

Eliphaz's name means "God is victorious." He made his home in Teman, a town located in Edom. Edom is the land that lies between the southern border of Israel and the Gulf of Aqaba. Later the descendants of Esau settled there. Eliphaz always spoke first. This indicates that he was the oldest and most prominent of the three men. The Scriptures provide no details about his life or family. He was the kindest of the three friends. Before coming to see Job, Eliphaz had had a dream that affected him greatly (4:12-21) and likely set the tone for all three of his speeches. Eliphaz believed that all suffering was punishment for sin. Therefore, in Eliphaz's mind, because Job was suffering greatly, he must have sinned grievously against God.

Eliphaz made three speeches in the Book of Job (chaps. 4–5; 15; and 22). In his first speech he treated Job kindly. He reminded Job that sinful men suffer for their sins, and he promised Job forgiveness and restoration if only Job would repent. In his second speech Eliphaz used sharper words. He expressed shock at Job's defense of his actions. He called on Job to repent and seek reconciliation with God—lest Job experience the terrible fate of the wicked. In his third speech Eliphaz cast off all restraint and accused Job of wickedness; nevertheless, Eliphaz ended his speech with praise for God's mercy on those who repent.

Eliphaz was a good man, a man of upright character and sympathy. Were he not kind and sympathetic, he would not have traveled many miles to see his friend. Still, his narrow and limited understanding of human suffering led him to misdiagnose Job's problem. When Job rejected his argument, Eliphaz responded with hateful words.[7]

BILDAD

Bildad's name may mean "son of Hadad," but this is not certain. Bildad lived in Shuah. The location of Shuah is unknown, but ancient Akkadian documents mention a district called Suhu, which was located on the Middle Euphrates River in what is now Iraq.[8]

As with Eliphaz, the Bible gives no information about Bildad's family. Most Bible commentators believe he was younger than Eliphaz, as it was customary for the oldest person to speak first. Bildad was a consummate traditionalist (8:8-10).

He expressed amazement that Job would question the traditional belief that suffering is the result of sin. The Book of Job includes three speeches by Bildad (chaps. 8; 18; and 25). In his first speech he acknowledged Job's children's sin, but Bildad also implied, not too subtly, that Job's sin may have contributed to the children's deaths. In his second speech Bildad discussed the awful fate of the wicked, and in his third speech he extolled the power of God and the sinful nature of human beings. His last speech was quite brief (chap. 25), maybe an indicator that Bildad had grown tired of talking to someone who would not agree with him. Exhibiting little concern for Job's feelings, Bildad's speeches instead focused on traditional theological claims.[9]

ZOPHAR

Zophar's name may mean "young bird" or "little bird." He came from Naamah. Although Naamah was almost certainly located east of the Jordan River, its exact location is still not known. The fact that Zophar spoke third suggests he was the youngest of the friends. He valued common sense and found no delight in many words (11:2). He showed little patience with Job. Like his friends, Zophar focused on Job's disobedience as the cause of his suffering. He went further than the friends, though, by suggesting that God had reduced Job's punishment.

The Book of Job records only two speeches by Zophar (chaps. 11; 20), though some commentators suggest that a portion of chapter 27 might be Zophar's third speech. The Hebrew text in that chapter is quite complex. In his speeches Zophar insisted that Job must have sinned; otherwise, he would not be suffering. Zophar came to the discussion with preconceived ideas, and he refused to adjust his thinking to Job's situation.[10]

EVALUATION

The Bible says Eliphaz, Bildad, and Zophar came to comfort Job. How well did they do? Job gave them a bad evaluation. He declared that they were "miserable comforters" (16:2, HCSB). Surely they meant well, but they made Job feel even worse than he did before their arrival.

Job's friends did some things right, though. They did visit Job, which was good. Many persons will avoid those who are grieving. Second, they sat with Job in silence for seven days. Often silence is healing. Many times one's presence is more helpful than one's words. Third, they expressed their opinions to Job personally. They did not talk behind his back.

Still, they failed completely in their efforts to help Job. Why did they fail? They failed because they held these convictions: (1) All suffering is the result of sin. (2) God punishes each act of sin with a penalty that corresponds to the gravity of the sin. (3) Suffering is proof of personal guilt. These ideas prevented them from understanding Job and his problem.

Not surprisingly, the three friends struggled to understand suffering. Four thousand years later we still wrestle with this issue. Truly, some suffering is the result of sin, but in Job's case the friends' assumptions were wrong. The Book of Job presents a new understanding of suffering. Not all suffering is the result of sin. Sometimes the innocent do suffer in this life. However, "suffering may be used as a means of demonstrating the faith of the saints, strengthening the faith of the saints, and extending the influence of the saints." That which can easily be overlooked may be one of the most hope-filled lessons from the book: "Suffering, faithfully endured, defeats Satan."[11]

Adapted from J. Mark Terry, "Job's Friends: Models of Compassion?" *Biblical Illustrator*, Fall 2005, 17-19.

One of the most hope-filled lessons
✗ from Job: "suffering, faithfully ✗
endured, defeats Satan."

* Frailty of man vs God's amazing
  grace to transform us.
* High view of God should result in
  a high view of self

* Questioning God : questions that
  come from desperation, confusion
  & sincere wonder are welcomed
  by the Lord.   But DON'T
  question his character!

Relational Take-Aways:

Eliphaz: you deserve this!

Bildad: your children sinned
       so they deserved to die!

Zophar: your talk to idle

• Job: You don't really know God!

• Job: gave friends another chance
       Job 17:10

Proverbs 27:6

Job 13:15 Job 1:9-11; Job 2:4-5 Job 14:14-15

Satan taunts Job: argues w/ God

    No matter what, I will not curse
Him.

"The veil gets thinner when we suffer."

When your life is falling apart, it
is Jesus who will hold you together.
Col 1:15-17

Pain of recovery is worse
than the thing that caused
the pain.

Recovery is equal to the degree you withdraw from God.

Video sessions available for purchase
or rent at www.LifeWay.com/Job

What you don't reveal, God cannot heal.

DISCUSSION QUESTIONS:

What one thing from the video teaching was new or interesting to you?

What does Lisa mean when she says that when we go through pain and suffering the veil between us and God becomes thinner? How has this been your experience?

When was a time someone you considered a friend added to your pain, rather than comforted you in your pain? How did you respond to that friend?

Is there a friendship you've given up on because your friend disappointed you? Explain. What do you think about giving them another chance?

When has a friend lovingly wounded you to help you see the truth?

Is there a friend to whom you need to lovingly speak hard truth? What's holding you back?

Are you surprised Job was able to remain faithful to the Lord despite his situation? Explain. Do you think you would have been able to do the same? Why or why not?

How does remembering the hope of what's ahead for us help us deal with what we are presently walking through?

3

THE EXPULSIVE POWER OF THE CROSS WITH REGARD TO PRETENSE

READING ASSIGNMENT:

Read Job 12–17 before the next video teaching time. Feel free to read the passage in sections (maybe one chapter at a time). If possible, try to read through all six chapters at least twice so that the meaning behind these words really sinks in.

MY STORY

Although I never heard "God will be disappointed in you if you don't pull yourself up by your bootstraps" in a sermon—at least not verbatim—I'd seen it demonstrated by adult church-goers so consistently that by the time I was in the first grade the scaffolding of my budding theology included a firm belief in self-sufficiency and optimism. I sincerely thought sad = bad. So I learned how to wear a happy expression and speak with a happy inflection even when sadness lurked beneath my emotional surface like a great white shark in a cold, dark sea.

Of course every now and then emotional sharks aren't content to slink around below the surface without biting. Which happened when I was sophomore in high school and the migraines I'd been having for a year or two worsened to the point of causing me to have blackouts and get violently sick every couple of weeks. After I lost consciousness at track practice one afternoon, Mom raced me to a neurologist who immediately had me admitted to a hospital because I had multiple symptoms of a brain tumor.

Fortunately after several days and a battery of tests, including a full psych consult, I was diagnosed as having a build up of cerebrospinal fluid behind my optic nerve, not a brain tumor or anything else life threatening. Other than dealing with the extreme awkwardness of several relatives sobbing uncontrollably in my hospital room after hovering outside the doorway and talking with Mom in hushed tones (The women in our family aren't always adept at dealing with sad, but we are quite gifted at drama.), that four-day hospital stay wasn't as grim as my family initially feared.

However, it didn't seem to be very beneficial or conclusive either. After explaining my condition to Mom, the neurologist declared ominously that besides a potentially fatal operation that involved installing a shunt in my head, which *might* help drain the excess fluid or putting me on powerful, anti-seizure meds, there was no other viable treatment. He added dismissively that there was a chance it would resolve itself after the hormonal fluctuations of puberty leveled out. Then he ended the consultation by sternly cautioning me against competitive athletics, being outside in the sun, and eating cheese or nuts. (Of course even then I knew that being a pale, lethargic couch potato bereft of chips and queso was far worse than a little fainting and projectile vomiting every now and then—so I was not a submissive patient. Fortunately by my freshman year in college the keeling and retching had become only a rare occurrence.)

I'd all but forgotten about that hospital stay until I was in my early forties and my counselor and I were excavating some of the bigger hills of my adolescence when I remembered an alarming, thoroughly-dismissed-at-the-time symptom from that long-ago health scare. I recalled it vividly because I'd heard mom tell this story numerous times when I was in my teens and twenties. While I was in the hospital a child psychiatrist met with me—as part of their normal protocol at the time when treating a minor—to ascertain whether he thought there were any signs of child abuse or mental illness. Following our two-hour visit he sat down with Mom to go over his evaluation. Once he'd explained that he found no signs of physical abuse or psychosis, he closed my file, took off his glasses, rubbed the bridge of his nose, and said soberly, "Mrs. Angel, Lisa is either the most happy, well-adjusted child I've ever met in my life, or she is in deep emotional pain."

Every time my dear mama got to the end of that story at a family gathering or while discussing me *in front of me* with a grocery store clerk or a saleslady behind the makeup counter in the mall, her voice would rise triumphantly because she regarded the psychiatrist's statement as proof that I was the happiest, most well-adjusted child in the history of the universe.

It took me two and a half decades to realize that the compassionate doctor was trying to tell my mom I was a pretty, little liar—that my mirth was mostly a mirage. Unfortunately by the time I was a teenager we'd already been pretending for so long that I suppose it felt safer to just keep dog-paddling on the surface instead of diving deep enough to deal with the sharks. And while young adulthood brought with it the growing awareness that the painful knots in my soul stemmed from childhood wounds I had no idea how to deal with them. So when I graduated from college, took a job in youth ministry, and became a "professional" Christian, I felt like I had no choice but to suppress any "bad" feelings and smile. Eventually I became a master happy doppelgänger.[1]

You've probably heard the platitude "Just fake it till you make it!" And maybe, like me, you've even adopted it as a strategy to survive difficult seasons. But I can promise you from decades of personal experience that the only thing faking makes is more of an emotional mess. Pretending you don't feel something doesn't get rid of the emotion. Instead, driving what we perceive to be sad, bad, or scary feelings deeper into the recesses of our souls may cause other problems to pop out—such as insincerity, isolation, depression, and the inability to experience true intimacy with others and with God.

These are exactly the kinds of problems Job candidly pointed out in Eliphaz, Bildad, and Zophar.

> What kind of people and/or situations make it more difficult for you to be utterly authentic? Explain your answer.

"Know-it-all" types
overly yoking
overly religious

Read John 4:1-26,39.

Obviously the fact that Jesus knew this woman's entire story—including her hurtful and humiliating history with men—and loved her anyway had a huge impact on the woman at the well. She not only put her hope in Him, but she shared her testimony with her community prompting *many* to believe in Jesus!

> How do you feel about Jesus knowing every single thing there is to know about you? Does His intimate knowledge of your *whole* story inspire you to share your testimony with others the way she did? If so, please share a recent experience of doing so!

Read Proverbs 27:19 below:

As water reflects the face,
so the heart reflects the person.

"The Hebrew [text] could be more literally rendered, 'Like the water, the face to the face, so the heart of the man to the man.'"[2] Some interpret this second line to mean that you can see your inner self reflected in the face of a friend or those closest to you.[3]

How often do you gaze at yourself in a relational kind of mirror—that is, when have you considered your emotional wellness based on the kind of people you surround yourself with?

In view of your current closest relationships, would you characterize yourself as being in robust emotional health, relative emotional health, relative emotional sickness, or grave emotional sickness? Explain.

JOB'S STORY

As has been mentioned before, the positions three stooges espouse aren't always heretical. Much of what they have to say about the relationship between God and man is theologically sound. What makes their sermons so hard to swallow is that they don't practice what they preach—like me for far too long, Job's friends are gifted fakers.

Job responds candidly to their counsel:

> Look, my eyes have seen all this;
> my ears have heard and understood it.
> Everything you know, I also know;
> I am not inferior to you.
> Yet I prefer to speak to the Almighty
> and argue my case before God.
> *You use lies like plaster;*
> *you are all worthless healers.*
> If only you would shut up
> and let that be your wisdom!
>
> Hear now my argument,
> and listen to my defense.
> *Would you testify unjustly on God's behalf*
> *or speak deceitfully for him?*
> Would you show partiality to him
> or argue the case in his defense?
> Would it go well if he examined you?
> *Could you deceive him as you would deceive a man?*
> Surely he would rebuke you
> if you secretly showed partiality.
> Would God's majesty not terrify you?
> Would his dread not fall on you?
> *Your memorable sayings are proverbs of ash;*
> *your defenses are made of clay.*
>
> JOB 13:1-12, *EMPHASIS MINE*

I have heard many things like these.
You are all miserable comforters.
Is there no end to your empty words?
What provokes you that you continue testifying?
If you were in my place I could also talk like you.
I could string words together against you
and shake my head at you.
Instead, I would encourage you with my mouth,
and the consolation from my lips would bring relief.

JOB 16:2-5, *EMPHASIS MINE*

While I was in the process of adopting Missy, a dear friend—also the adoptive mom of an HIV-positive child that she and her husband brought home several years before I began our journey—soberly warned me about disingenuous, religious people. She said, "Be careful about throwing the pearl of your and Missy's relationship before the swine of Southern façades. Most of the women you know from church will praise you initially for being such a 'good' person by rescuing a brown baby from certain death in a developing country. They'll throw all kinds of accolades in your direction. But just wait until you actually bring Missy home and she goes from being a picture on their refrigerator to a real-live student in the same classrooms as their children. Your Christian friends' real colors will come out when they choose whether or not to invite your beautifully scarred little girl to their kid's pool party."

I didn't really know how to respond to her unvarnished candor. I wondered if maybe she'd developed a root of bitterness over one bad apple of a mom who was less-than-gracious after they brought their baby home. But then a few months after Missy came home we bumped into another mother and her daughter—whom I've known for years from church circles—at Costco®. After a polite greeting, we introduced our suddenly shy daughters who are exactly the same age. I watched that mama's eyes shift and break contact with mine as her countenance hardened into a fake smile. Then I listened in sad dismay while her voice rose into a perky falsetto as she prattled something along the lines of, "When my schedule isn't so crazy maybe we can get our girls together sometime for a playdate!" all the while sticking her arm out like a human guardrail and then slowly sweeping her baby girl backward, away from Missy. Then my straightforward friend's cautionary advice came rushing back to me.

That's the gist of Job's experience with his pretend friends too:

> You use lies like plaster;
> you are all worthless healers.
>
> JOB 13:4

In other words, *you cover up your true feelings with dishonest prattling, and your fake compassion is utterly useless in easing my pain.*

> Your memorable sayings are proverbs of ash;
> your defenses are made of clay.
>
> JOB 13:12

In other words, *the spiritual platitudes you've been quoting to me are as useless and temporal as the ash at the bottom of our fireplace or the gum on the bottom of my boot.*

> Is there no end to your empty words?
>
> JOB 16:3

In other words, *please shut your trap because every hokey, disingenuous word that falls out of your big mouth is landing on my last nerve.*

I deeply regret having presented a false self to friends and family members for years. Many of them were emotionally mature and secure enough to love me well, warts and all. Yet they were rendered inept in their desire to enjoy a real relationship with me by my strong stiff-arm of pretense. That's one of the reasons I'm both encouraged and convicted by Job's pleas for his friends to be more authentic, as well as the way he questions the validity of their relationship with God in light of their discernable deception (Job 13:6-11).

While pondering this phase of Job's journey, I vividly remembered this passage from *Ruthless Trust*, a book written by Brennan Manning that I read in the "laid-bare" phase of my own journey to authenticity:

> The bromides, platitudes, and exhortations to trust God from nominal
> believers who have never visited the valley of desolation are not only
> useless, they are textbook illustrations of unmitigated gall. Only someone
> who has been there, who has drunk the dregs of our cup of pain, who
> has experienced the existential loneliness and alienation of the human

condition, dares whisper the name of the Holy to our unspeakable distress. Only that witness is credible; only that love is believable.[4]

Only that witness is credible; only that love is believable.[5] Wow, that's more than enough motivation to take off our masks of pretense, isn't it?

Is there anyone, other than your parents or spouse, who truly knows the "real you"—warts and all—and loves you anyway? If so, what does that person's almost (only God has the ability to express *perfectly unconditional* love!) unconditional affection mean to you?

Would anyone say that you know him/her completely and love him/her fully? If so, how have you practically lived out this affection for that person?

Read 2 Corinthians 1:3-7. Why do you think *empathy* is more effective at comforting people in pain than *sympathy*?

Empathy 7 you understand &
share their feelings/

KEY POINTS TO PONDER IN JOB'S STORY

Losing his children, his livelihood, his reputation, and his physical health left Job marked with tangible and intangible scars. These ridges on both his body and soul proved he'd endured great pain. Unfortunately, the people who remained in his life—his wife and friends—regarded Job's emotional and physical blemishes as unsightly, even ugly. But I believe God has a wholly different perspective about the scars His children have earned. I think He regards them as beauty marks.

I got to hang out with Wonder Woman recently. Well, not Wonder Woman *exactly*. Her name is Lori, not Gal Gadot (the actress who portrayed Wonder Woman in the 2017 blockbuster film of the same name). But she's incredibly brave despite her lack of knee-high red boots and a cape. Lori just passed the three-month mark of being clean from methamphetamines after an eight year addiction that culminated in her conviction for illegal drug possession and armed robbery charges.

Unlike most of the women I meet at The Next Door (a six-month, faith-based residential program that provides recovery support services for women conquering their addictions to alcohol and drugs), Lori looks younger than her age. (She's twenty-three.) The first time we met she was wearing a hoodie sweatshirt with a popular logo emblazoned on the front, torn jeans, and metallic nail polish. As a matter of fact, if I'd seen her strolling through the mall or giggling with her girlfriends at Starbucks®, I would've assumed she was a happy-go-lucky college student. It wasn't until she pushed up the sleeves of her sweatshirt, revealing long, ragged scars from shooting up, that the tragic reality of her former life became apparent.

Because I've had the privilege of volunteering with several addiction recovery programs, much of Lori's story is achingly familiar. She grew up in a very poor family in a very small town. One of her parents moonlighted as a mean-spirited bully, claiming to be "knocking the stupid out of her" when smacking Lori around. Of course, Lori wasn't stupid at all. Despite the regular beatings she endured at home, she excelled in school. She made the honor roll and the cheerleading squad. After an emotional commitment to Christ at a youth rally, she became an outspoken Christian leader on campus. However, when her parents divorced and she became the sole possession of her abuser, Lori's world caved in. She eventually ran away from home and moved in with her boyfriend. He introduced her to methamphetamines, which numbed the searing pain of the compound fractures in her heart. And the rest, as they say, is history. Horrible, awful, gut-wrenching history. That is until God intervened with a team of Tennessee-based federal agents wearing flak jackets. Lori's voice brightened when she shared the part of her story where those law enforcement officers burst into her trailer to arrest her. She looked up at me through her bangs and grinned. Then she said with newfound confidence, "Miss Lisa, I know God ordained the exact timing of my drug bust, because I'd planned to commit suicide that afternoon. If those cops hadn't come when they did, I wouldn't be sitting here today."

Before I left, we talked about the Bible study we'll be doing every Wednesday night for the next three months. After that, she has to report to prison to serve what will likely be a reduced sentence of about eighteen months. When we hugged good-bye, she whispered that she wants to be a Bible teacher too when she gets out. I whispered back that her testimony will plunge the divine sword into Satan's chest even deeper and be used to set captives free. Lori's recovery will be a day-by-day, uphill journey, but I can totally picture her a few years from now standing in front of a room filled with wide-eyed young girls hanging on every word of her redemption story.

The older I get, the more convinced I am that admittedly flawed sinners are the most credible witnesses of the gospel. Blemished believers can't *fake* moral superiority like Job's less-than-genuine buddies did. Our scars make it glaringly apparent that we couldn't protect ourselves from harm. Authentic Christian warriors with scabby knees, bruised hearts, and even track-marked arms, who sometimes stumble yet always grab onto the arm of His Spirit in order to stand up again and again, exemplify the redemptive power of divine grace. We prove how miraculous and restorative the love of God really is. We *know* we can't make it by ourselves and can only *keep ourselves together* because of the miraculous redemption King Jesus provided for us on the cross!

Job was able to prophesy about the cross of Christ at least one thousand years before the event because God made the veil thin during his season of honest agony. I can't help but wonder what you and I would be able to speak powerfully about if we had the courage to be gut-level honest about our desperate need for God's comfort.

In his book, *Ruthless Trust*, Brennan Manning also wrote,

On the last day, Jesus will look us over not for medals, diplomas, or honors, but for scars.[6]

What are a few of the scars you could show Him now? Would you describe all of your scars as "badges of honor"? Why or why not?

Google the name "Arthur Blessitt" to read the true story of a man who's spent the last fifty years[7] carrying a twelve-foot wooden cross all over the world[8] (He's "cross-walked" in over three hundred countries!) as a way to share the gospel of Jesus Christ.[9]

What do you think about this unconventional method of ministry? Why do you think replicas of the cross—whether a wooden, life-sized version like the one Arthur Blessitt carries or a metal crucifix worn as jewelry—are inspirational symbols to millions of people when the original cross was the Roman equivalent of a modern-day death chamber?

It shows our devotion to Christ

Read Matthew 16:24-26. How do you practically apply Jesus' admonition in your life?

Jesus must be first in my life — avoid Satan & sinly deeds.

KEY CHARACTER IN JOB'S STORY

OK, I need to start with a confession: the character we're about to consider wasn't technically in Job's story. However, her story took place around 1100 BC so who knows but what she went to high school with Job. And her name was Hannah:

> There was a man from Ramathaim-zophim in the hill country of Ephraim. His name was Elkanah son of Jeroham, son of Elihu, son of Tohu, son of Zuph, an Ephraimite. He had two wives, the first named Hannah and the second Peninnah. Peninnah had children, but Hannah was childless. This man would go up from his town every year to worship and to sacrifice to the LORD of Armies at Shiloh, where Eli's two sons, Hophni and Phinehas, were the LORD's priests.
>
> Whenever Elkanah offered a sacrifice, he always gave portions of the meat to his wife Peninnah and to each of her sons and daughters. But he gave a double portion to Hannah, for he loved her even though the LORD had kept her from conceiving. Her rival would taunt her severely just to provoke her, because the LORD had kept Hannah from conceiving. Year after year, when she went up to the LORD's house, her rival taunted her in this way. Hannah would weep and would not eat. "Hannah, why are you crying?" her husband Elkanah would ask. "Why won't you eat? Why are you troubled? Am I not better to you than ten sons?"
>
> On one occasion, Hannah got up after they ate and drank at Shiloh. The priest Eli was sitting on a chair by the doorpost of the LORD's temple. Deeply hurt, Hannah prayed to the LORD and wept with many tears. Making a vow, she pleaded, "LORD of Armies, if you will take notice of your servant's affliction, remember and not forget me, and give your servant a son, I will give him to the LORD all the days of his life, and his hair will never be cut."
>
> While she continued praying in the LORD's presence, Eli watched her mouth. Hannah was praying silently, and though her lips were moving, her voice could not be heard. Eli thought she was drunk and said to her, "How long are you going to be drunk? Get rid of your wine!"
>
> "No, my lord," Hannah replied. "I am a woman with a broken heart. I haven't had any wine or beer; I've been pouring out my heart before the

LORD. Don't think of me as a wicked woman; I've been praying from the depth of my anguish and resentment."

Eli responded, "Go in peace, and may the God of Israel grant the request you've made of him."

"May your servant find favor with you," she replied. Then Hannah went on her way; she ate and no longer looked despondent.

1 SAMUEL 1:1-18

I'm so glad this historical tale clarifies that Hannah was emoting greatly in God's house, even though her feelings were on the sad end of the emotional spectrum because she was grieving her infertility. Frankly, I believe one of the biggest fallacies perpetrated in communities of faith is that the closer we get to Jesus the more we need to keep a lid on it. That deep spirituality is revealed in social propriety, which typically means pulling a polite façade over sad or "bad" feelings.

I received tons of congregational stink-eyes for being a greatly emoting church kid when I was growing up. By the time I was five or six years old, I thought I was probably destined to stand facing the corner in God's house in heaven. The adults around me had made it crystal clear He preferred socially-appropriate kids who didn't ask too many direct questions in Sunday School, bellow happily when they sang in the children's choir, or turn exuberant cartwheels in the church foyer. I learned the hard way that being too honest or too demonstrative when it came to Jesus was right up there with the big, brow-raising Baptist no-nos such as drinking, dancing, and tattoos.

One of the wisest moves I've made as a mom is to teach Missy the opposite of what was tacitly endorsed and enforced when I was her age. I don't want her to ever feel like she has to put a lid on her emotions.

And as best as I can understand the redemptive narrative of Scripture, I don't think God wants His kids to either. Case in point, instead of ignoring Hannah's honest plea or lecturing her for shattering the sanctimony of the temple with her overtly emotional display, God rewarded her honest angst:

The next morning Elkanah and Hannah got up early to worship before the LORD. Afterward, they returned home to Ramah. Then Elkanah was intimate with his wife Hannah, and the LORD remembered her. After some time, Hannah conceived and gave birth to a son. She named him Samuel, because she said, "I requested him from the LORD."

1 SAMUEL 1:19-20

If you've been shushed by Christian killjoys like I have, be encouraged, Hannah's and Job's stories prove that propriety is not a prerequisite for God's favor, nor is it a spiritual gift!

YOUR STORY

Read Job 9:32-33; 16:19-21; 19:25-27; and 33:23.

As an homage to the above Messianic references in the Book of Job, we're going to spend some time meditating on the significance of Christ's sacrifice on the cross by walking through The Stations of the Cross. This is common practice for Catholics during Lent but not nearly as common in Protestant circles.

First of all, get one or two of the more crafty chicks in your Bible study to create fourteen unique images that correspond to all fourteen stations. Or, if your group is severely lacking in women who enjoy roaming the aisles of Hobby Lobby®, you can always download images from the Internet. (There are actually some good ones on The Stations of the Cross websites for children!)

Next, create posters for each of the following stations—including the station number, title, and biblical passage(s)—on a large piece of construction paper or poster board. If possible, laminate each poster so you can leave them up in an outdoor environment.

STATION	TITLE	SCRIPTURE
Station 1	Jesus prays on the Mount of Olives.	Luke 22:39-46
Station 2	Jesus is betrayed and arrested.	Luke 22:47-48
Station 3	Jesus is condemned by the Sanhedrin.	Luke 22:66-71
Station 4	Peter betrays Jesus.	Luke 22:54-62
Station 5	Jesus is judged by Pilate.	Luke 23:13-25
Station 6	Jesus is scourged and crowned with thorns.	Luke 22:63-65; John 19:2-3
Station 7	Jesus takes up the cross.	John 19:6,15-17

STATION	TITLE	SCRIPTURE
Station 8	Simon of Cyrene helps Jesus carry His cross.	Luke 23:26
Station 9	Jesus meets the women of Jerusalem.	Luke 23:27-31
Station 10	Jesus is crucified.	Luke 23:33-34,46-47
Station 11	Jesus promises His kingdom to the believing thief.	Luke 23:39-43
Station 12	Jesus talks to His mother and disciple from the cross.	John 19:25-27
Station 13	Jesus dies on the cross.	Luke 23:44-47
Station 14	Jesus is placed in the tomb.	Luke 23:50-54; Mark 15:42-47

Once all fourteen station posters have been made, find an outdoor space where you can create a walk that begins with the first station and ends with the fourteenth. Church green spaces or large private yards work great if they have a linear fence or enough trees to affix all of the stations with thumbtacks. You can attach the stations to long yard stakes/poles in the absence of a fence or trees.

Next, enlist someone to nail two boards together in the shape of a cross and cover it with chicken wire using a staple gun or small, u-shaped nails. Then stand the wooden cross in the same general area as the fourteen stations.

Before this event, procure enough fresh, long-stemmed carnations, daisies, or roses for each person in your group to have one.

Finally, when the time comes to experience The Stations of the Cross with your Bible study buddies, begin with a group prayer. Then direct everyone to meander slowly through all fourteen stations at their own pace. Encourage them to take time to read the Bible passage listed for each station and meditate on what Jesus experienced. Instead of ending at the fourteenth station, complete the walk at the cross. There each participant will insert her flower into the chicken wire, symbolizing the abundant life Jesus provides through His sacrificial death. If someone in your group is musical, it would be lovely to end your activity with a worship song or two. And if it's possible for each member of your group to purchase (or make) a cross for someone else, exchanging those crosses with each other as a way of "sealing" the experience of walking through The Stations of the Cross can be a very meaningful gesture.

When our Bible study group did this, there was such a strong, positive response in the community that we decided to leave everything up for several more days—which is where the lamination came in handy because it rained that week! We also included a water bucket filled with long-stemmed carnations beside the cross. Our makeshift stations ended up being used by so many families (many of whom we didn't even know) that by the end of the week our cross was completely covered in flowers!

If conducting the walk through the stations is not possible in an outdoor setting, consider setting it up inside your church or in a large home.

IS GOD TRYING TO RUIN MY LIFE?

BY MARTHA LAWLEY

Surely I'm not the only one who has wondered about God's intentions when life gets painfully hard. Perhaps your questions are more specific: *Is God trying to ruin my ministry, my marriage, my career, or my happiness?* We all well know that life this side of heaven is difficult. But sometimes we experience circumstances that are more than hard—circumstances that knock us down and drain the life right out of us. In these extraordinary seasons, we are often left to wonder what God is doing. For me, wanting to understand can be as powerful as wanting it all to go away.

Many of my truly difficult and overwhelming circumstances have involved my health. The past twenty years have been a roller coaster journey of both long- and short-term health challenges. But these have paled in comparison to the past twelve months. This intense season of physical suffering included two biopsies, another spinal fusion, extensive physical therapy, cataract surgeries, and a retinal reattachment surgery. During the retina reattachment surgery in January, a gas bubble was inserted in my eye to aid my recovery. The gas bubble works like a cast holding the newly repaired retina in place. However, the bubble has prevented me from flying or even driving for the past two months. The emergency surgery occurred while on vacation at sea level. I live at an altitude of more than four thousand feet. I'm writing to you in my eighth week of exile. So I couldn't help but wonder in the midst of all this—not out loud, but in my mind—*Is God trying to ruin my life?* If that question disappoints you, I am sorry.

While not the best question to ask, it was a place to start, and God used it. He used it to teach me new truths and to remind me of much I already knew. He opened the door to greater understanding of who He is and of His great love for me. He gave me the opportunity to see more clearly and believe more deeply. Here are four of the most important things He has planted even deeper into my soul.

1. ASK BETTER QUESTIONS.

The Bible gives me encouragement that God is OK with sincere questions. But I believe He invites us to ask better questions. My questioning God about ruining my life reveals how self-focused I had become. ("Why this? Why me? Why now?") I'm learning that the better questions always focus on God—who He is and what He can do. Questions like, "How are you going to use this to advance the gospel in and through me?" (see Phil. 1:12). "How can I display Your great strength in my great weakness?" (see 2 Cor. 12:9-10). Asking better questions shifts my focus back to God.

Adapted from Martha Lawley, "Is God Trying to Ruin My Life?" *LifeWay Ministry to Women Blog*, March 7, 2018.

2. SEEK WISDOM FROM ABOVE.

God invites us to seek His wisdom (Jas. 1:5). The world does not have the answers to our questions. Only God can provide reliable answers to our questions. God has already provided all we need to know in His Word and through His Spirit. I love the Bible, but on my most difficult days, it can be a struggle for me to let God's Word speak into my life. However this is when I most need these wonderful words of life—words that declare God's love, reveal His motives, and describe His ways. Prayer is another way God reminds me of His truth. Praying is not difficult for me in times of hardship, but listening often is. God continues to use His Word and prayer to refocus my life in difficult times.

3. KEEP TRUSTING GOD— HIS MOTIVES, HIS PLAN (HEB. 12:1-3).

This is a continuing battle for me, and one I don't always win. These past twelve months have been filled with moments of desperate confession, "I do believe, but help my unbelief!" (Mark 9:24). God continues to graciously invite us to count each blessing and discover His loving care in each gift. As incredibly hard as this season has been, I have so much to be thankful for. Stopping to remember and name each blessing reminds me that God has been there each step of the way.

4. DISCOVER THE BEAUTY IN BROKENNESS (2 COR. 12:9).

God reveals His power in our brokenness. All I'm currently going through is an opportunity to reveal God—His power, His glory, His love. Only God can make our lives more beautiful for having been broken (Jas. 1:2-4). Recognizing the greater purposes in my struggles—knowing not one minute of my suffering has been in vain—helps me persevere. *Lord, help me!*

What about you? What is God teaching you right now? How would you encourage someone in the midst of an incredibly difficult season?

Pray, Pray & pray some more.

Recognize the season, knowing (having hope) that spring always comes.

Lean on your Christian friends. Let them in; let them hold & comfort you.

On the last day, Jesus will look us over for scars... pg 70

Flawed sinners are the most credible witnesses of the gospel

scars are beauty marks in God's eyes

DISCUSSION QUESTIONS:

What one thing from the video teaching was new or interesting to you?

Share a time when you were in pain and despair, longing to be heard. Why is it important to be heard when we are in pain and suffering?

Do you believe that God always hears you? Why or why not?

Lisa says that Job not only longed to be heard, but he also longed to be held. What do you think she meant by that?

Share a time when you experienced God holding you, circling you with His affection.

How can God be both accuser and Redeemer?

What does it mean for God to be your Redeemer? Are you able to still have hope that He is your Redeemer even in the midst of your deepest pain? Explain.

4

THE SERENITY
OF SURRENDER

READING ASSIGNMENT:

Peruse Job 18–31 between now and watching the next video teaching. Feel free to read the passage in sections (maybe one chapter at a time). If possible, try to read through all the chapters at least twice so that the meaning behind these words begins to sink in.

MY STORY

Recently Missy, Kylie (an angel disguised as a twenty-something blonde who is my part-time nanny/personal assistant and full-time friend), and I had a posterior-numbing twelve-hour road trip returning home from a wonderful women's conference in south Alabama. Of course, it should've only been seven hours, but we made one rather lengthy pit stop in Troy, AL. First we had to eat at Crowe's, which has been serving the best fried chicken since I went to undergrad at Troy University more than thirty years ago. Then I had to walk my polite—albeit completely unimpressed— eight-year-old around Troy's campus in the drizzling rain while I shrieked things like, "Baby, this is the cafeteria where we ate our meals when I was in school here!" and "Miss, see that old building behind those magnolia trees? That's the gym where I played college volleyball!" and "Honey, that pond over there is where I got dunked when I pledged Kappa Delta!"

Since Kylie and Missy patiently endured that trip down memory lane, I felt led to stop again a mere twenty minutes down the road in order to drag them down every single aisle at Sikes and Kohn's Country Mall. This was—and evidently still is—*the* place to shop between Troy and Montgomery. It's where my college girlfriends and I got all our preppy accoutrements such as crisp twill khakis, pink button-downs, and green belts with white sailboats when we were perky, poofy-haired coeds back in the eighties. The fact that we ran into some old friends while we were perusing their once-a-year shoe sale was the cherry on top of my sweet nostalgia sundae. And *then*, as if we hadn't had enough fun already, we got to hang out with Mr. Sikes himself, plus pray for not one but *two* women in the store (who recognized Missy from social media) who were going through difficulties. I'm telling you, we had ourselves a mini-revival right there in the middle of that quintessentially southern retail superstore. But I also have to tell you that all the excitement and reminiscing sapped my common sense just like leaving your car lights on drains your battery, because I accidentally left my wallet in a gas station at our very last pit stop!

Of course, I didn't notice it was missing until the next morning when I picked up my purse before heading out the door and thought, *Wow, this sure is light.* Then I got that terrible feeling in the pit of my stomach when I began rummaging around in my purse and couldn't find my wallet. I realized it could be at any one of the three or four potty/coffee/gas stops we made in Alabama and Tennessee—that was after buying seven pairs of shoes that were too cheap to pass up at Sikes and Kohn's. (I know, I know, seven pairs of shoes, but most of them really were for Missy!) It took thirty minutes of retracing our steps and a few frustrating phone calls before finally discovering where I'd left it. Thankfully, someone had graciously turned it in. But before turning it in they had ungraciously rifled through it and taken the four hundred dollars cash that was in it.

I know, being robbed of four hundred dollars from a wallet I'd left in a bathroom stall in the middle of nowhere was *totally* my fault—and probably served me right for buying so many shoes even if they were practically free—but I still felt somewhat deflated when we drove back to that last pit stop to reclaim it. I thought, *Ugh, I've got a million things to do today. The last thing I need to be doing is spending half the day chasing down my wallet and feeling guilty about losing four hundred hard-earned bucks.* After driving in silence for a few minutes, Missy asked me if I was sad. I said, "Just a little bit, baby." When she asked why, I explained that someone had taken our money without asking—which left both of us feeling a little subdued. We stopped a few minutes later to grab some sub sandwiches for lunch. As I was pulling money out of my pocket to pay for our food, a woman who was grinning from ear-to-ear held one hand up, motioning for me to pause. Then, before I even realized what she was doing, she swiped her credit card to buy our meal. She laughed at my momentary bewilderment and went on to explain that she'd been really encouraged by my Bible studies and was tickled to meet Missy and me. She said buying our lunch was the least she could do to thank us for the spiritual blessings we'd brought into her life.

I couldn't stop smiling as we rode down the interstate, happily snacking on free subs en route to pick up my mostly empty wallet. (Thankfully the wallet returner/cash thief had chosen to leave my driver's license and credit cards.) Then when Missy asked sincerely,

"Mama, was that lady at the sandwich place an angel?" I couldn't help laughing before replying, "Maybe, baby. Maybe." Remember our discussion from the Week 1 teaching video about how the idea of deservedness isn't biblically sound? We reinforced that thought by looking at Matthew 5:45b:

> For he causes his sun to rise on the evil and the good,
> and sends rain on the righteous and the unrighteous.

After our teensy first-world problem was turned on its head by a generous sub shop cherub, I also couldn't help musing, *Instead of focusing on the inevitable rainfall in that verse, I want to focus on the inevitable sunshine.* In view of our perfect heavenly Father, who gives good gifts to His children (Matt. 7:11), even our deepest disappointments will ultimately prove to be simple gatekeepers for future delight. No matter how hard it's raining in our lives now, it's really only a thimbleful of liquid in the vast ocean of God's sovereignty. And may we not forget that in the divine template of eternity, this too shall pass.

What helped you turn a recent problem into a praise?

Read 2 Corinthians 4:17. How would you paraphrase this verse so that a child could understand it?

Problems pass away — heaven never will.

Which of your current hardships or heartaches is the easiest to describe as momentary and light? Which one of your current hardships or heartaches is difficult to imagine being momentary or temporary?

Would you describe your life currently as having more rainy days or more sunny days? Explain.

More sunny days, I am in a good place right now. My health is under the control & all is well. It actually scares me to write that! Why do I have to feel that the other shoe will drop...

JOB'S STORY

There's been so much agony in Job's words and so much contentiousness in his friends' words—when we read a few positive verses of praise in this middle section of discourse, it seems like a beautiful rainbow after a terrible storm. And some of the most delightful phraseology—after Job's glorious proclamation that his Redeemer lives in Job 19—can be found in Job 26 when he replies to Bildad's third speech. It's as if the rain over Job's life ceases for a while, and the sun pierces the darkness of his circumstances for a few long moments of radiant warmth that leaves him smiling with delight over who God is:

Then Job answered:

How you have helped the powerless
and delivered the arm that is weak!
How you have counseled the unwise
and abundantly provided insight!
With whom did you speak these words?
Whose breath came out of your mouth?

The departed spirits tremble
beneath the waters and all that inhabit them.
Sheol is naked before God,
and Abaddon has no covering.

He stretches the northern skies over empty space;
he hangs the earth on nothing.
He wraps up the water in his clouds,
yet the clouds do not burst beneath its weight.
He obscures the view of his throne,
spreading his cloud over it.
He laid out the horizon on the surface of the waters
at the boundary between light and darkness.
The pillars that hold up the sky tremble,
astounded at his rebuke.
By his power he stirred the sea,
and by his understanding he crushed Rahab.

By his breath the heavens gained their beauty;
his hand pierced the fleeing serpent.
These are but the fringes of his ways;
how faint is the word we hear of him!
Who can understand his mighty thunder?

JOB 26, *EMPHASIS MINE*

The overwhelming takeaway of Job's exultation in this chapter is that God is so completely all-powerful and majestic that His glory is beyond human comprehension! It's an oratory salute to the same Creator Job accuses of crushing him—the same Redeemer he demands to have a chat with and waggle his finger at because of what he perceives as unfair treatment. Job's turnabout is proof that human emotions can be an extremely fickle tour guide; therefore, they are not to be followed blindly.

Read Psalm 62. Much like Job, David seems to vacillate between woe and worship here. With which lines of the psalm do you most identify? Why?

8 Trust in him at all times...
Pour out your heart to him,
for God is our refuge.

In light of David's confession about finding rest in God alone, what's the most spiritually restful season you've ever experienced?

Right now

Reread Job 26. In light of Job's poetic imagery about God hanging the earth in empty space and wrapping seas around clouds, what metaphor(s) would you use to describe God's divine creative ability?

KEY POINTS TO PONDER IN JOB'S STORY

As tempting as it is to just relax and marinate for a while in this uplifting discourse after so much dreary dialogue, there are three facets in this sparkling jewel of a chapter that bear closer inspection:

"SHEOL IS NAKED BEFORE GOD, AND ABADDON HAS NO COVERING" (v. 6). To strip someone naked has often been used as a way of asserting dominance over a foe. It was a common tactic used by Nazi soldiers to dehumanize and humiliate Jewish prisoners during the Holocaust. And it continues today, based on recent UN accounts of Rohingya refugees who were forced to strip naked by their captors.[1] Job's use of the proper name "Abaddon" here, which is the same name the Book of Revelation gives Satan (Rev. 9:11),[2] reveals that God has stripped the enemy of our souls of his power and has complete dominion over him. That lying lizard will enjoy some small victories in the epic battle of good and evil we see playing out here on earth, but make no mistake about it, God. Is. In. Control. And the war has already been won. Job's visual here of Satan squirming naked and helpless before Almighty God reminds me of John's vision of the evil one as a defeated dragon:

> Then war broke out in heaven: Michael and his angels fought against the dragon. The dragon and his angels also fought, but he could not prevail, and there was no place for them in heaven any longer. So the great dragon was thrown out—the ancient serpent, who is called the devil and Satan, the one who deceives the whole world. He was thrown to earth, and his angels with him. Then I heard a loud voice in heaven say,
>
> The salvation and the power
> and the kingdom of our God
> and the authority of his Christ
> have now come,
> because the accuser of our brothers and sisters,
> who accuses them
> before our God day and night,
> has been thrown down.
> They conquered him
> by the blood of the Lamb
> and by the word of their testimony;
> for they did not love their lives
> to the point of death.

Therefore rejoice, you heavens,
and you who dwell in them!
Woe to the earth and the sea,
because the devil has come down to you
with great fury,
because he knows his time is short.

REVELATION 12:7-12

"BY HIS POWER HE STIRRED THE SEA, AND BY HIS UNDERSTANDING HE CRUSHED RAHAB" (v. 12).

The word *Rahab* doesn't refer to the Old Testament chick with the scarlet cord who saved the lives of two Jewish spies (Josh. 2). It is a reference to the mythical sea monster that represented Egypt, the Israelites' archenemy.[3] Therefore what Job is saying here is similar to the comprehensive, 360 degree blessing God gave Abram (later known as Abraham) in Genesis 12:

The LORD said to Abram:

Go out from your land,
your relatives,
and your father's house
to the land that I will show you.
I will make you into a great nation,
I will bless you,
I will make your name great,
and you will be a blessing.
I will bless those who bless you,
I will curse anyone who treats you with contempt,
and all the peoples on earth
will be blessed through you.

GENESIS 12:1-3, *EMPHASIS MINE*

God didn't just bless Abraham, He also vowed to curse anyone who treated him poorly. Which is kind of like God promising to meet all your financial needs, plus vowing to give anyone who steals money from your lost wallet a nasty case of full-body hives! And

Job 26:12 is prophetically accurate because it goes on to be fulfilled in Job's life when God chastises and punishes his "frenemies" Eliphaz, Bildad, and Zophar (Job 42:7-9).

"THESE ARE BUT THE FRINGES OF HIS WAYS" (v. 14a).

I love that Job uses "fringe" as a metaphor for God's power. It reminds me of how a very sick woman, who'd been suffering for twelve long years, was miraculously and instantaneously healed the moment she touched the fringe of Jesus' robe:

> And behold, a woman who had suffered from a discharge of blood for twelve years came up behind him and touched the fringe of his garment, for she said to herself, "If I only touch his garment, I will be made well." Jesus turned, and seeing her he said, "Take heart, daughter; your faith has made you well." And instantly the woman was made well.
>
> MATTHEW 9:20-22, ESV

This chapter of sunny clarity for Job—that occurs smack-dab in the middle of his crisis—is a refreshing reminder that no matter how hard the going gets:

- God has absolute dominion over the enemy of our souls.

- God has our best interests in mind, and He's got our backs.

- God has the power to heal our greatest infirmities without even lifting His pinkie.

  Read 1 Peter 5:8. What is the enemy trying to devour and destroy in this season of your life? How do you practically acknowledge God's authority over Satan in your story?

  My peace & serenity. Reminding myself that God clearly told me: "Abide in me!"

Read Isaiah 52:12. How was God your rear guard, or how did He have your back in your early years as a follower of Christ? How about recently?

He helped me escape myself & wrong choices.
He has sent me Christian friends that are people to emulate.

Read Matthew 9:18-26; Mark 5:21-43; Luke 8:40-56. These accounts tell the story of two desperate people. How did their words and actions express their desperation? Have you ever been that desperate for Jesus? Explain.

KEY CHARACTER IN JOB'S STORY

Probably like you, I'm sick and tired of Eliphaz, Bildad, and Zophar's sanctimonious shenanigans. So I'm going to cheat again and focus on a character who, like Hannah, was not technically in Job's story—but one who surely cheered him on from the cheap seats. The key characters we're going to consider this time are the psalmists. The Psalms were written over a timespan of almost one thousand years, from Moses' era (1400 BC) until the Southern Jews returned from captivity in Babylon (around 500 BC).[4] Since we don't know the exact date of Job's story, some of these worship songs—most of the Psalms were originally composed as "songs," so I like to think of the Psalter as God's iPod—may have been familiar to Job. Who knows but what he hummed a few of them while trying to drown out the on-going drivel of the three stooges!

Depending on which commentary you read or seminary professor you sit under, at least one third to half of all the psalms are classified as songs of *lament* or sad songs.[5] And with the exception of Psalm 88, sooner or later they all evolve into praise choruses.[6] Therefore, much like the way Job lifts his eyes from the depressing ruins of his life to gaze at God, the psalmists also penned tunes that herald how divine daybreaks follow the darkest nights.

One of my favorite modern-day psalmists, Michael Card, explained the connection between godly sorrow and celebration in his marvelous book, *A Sacred Sorrow*: "There is no worship without wilderness. There can be no worshipful joy of salvation until we have realized the lamentable wilderness of what we were saved from, until we begin to understand just what it cost Jesus to come and find us and be that perfect provision in the wilderness."[7] In other words, delight and despair are first cousins.

When the church I used to attend voted to build a new sanctuary, the senior pastor (a wonderful shepherd named Dr. Charles McGowan) insisted on having kneelers in front of each pew. In my experience, Christians tend to fuss about non-essential things like the color of the carpeting and the size of the pulpit, so of course more than a few grumbled about Charles's resolve for kneelers. They emailed him things like, "This is not an old-fashioned church. We're modern evangelicals. We shouldn't have anything that formal in the sanctuary." Several women stopped him in the foyer on Sunday mornings to complain, "Those silly things always catch my heels and cause me to trip when I'm trying to find a seat." Some of the grumpiest congregants argued, "What's next, smells and bells? If I wanted to kneel in church, I'd go to the cathedral downtown." Fortunately Charles was old enough and wise enough to ignore the naysayers and nitpickers. When the sanctuary was completed, velvet-covered kneelers were permanent fixtures.

I joined the leadership team at that church several years later, and I can't tell you how many times on a Monday afternoon or a Thursday morning, when the sanctuary was dark and empty, I'd walk in and find a place on one of those kneelers. I'd pray *Oh Father, please forgive me for having such a rotten attitude. I need You to cleanse my heart and renew my mind and help me not to think cuss words about church members.* Or, *Dear Lord, I'm sorry for worrying about what people think of me more than what You think of me. Please forgive me for bowing to the altar of human approval, and help me to walk in a way that honors You, no matter what anybody else thinks.* Or, *God, I'm such a goober. Remember what I asked You to forgive me for this morning? Well, I just did it again!* I'm pretty sure that after my six year stint on staff at that church they had to replace the velvet on a few kneelers because I'd worn it so thin.

I will always be grateful to my former pastor for his prescience, because I needed those kneelers. Bowing low in cognizance of God's power and majesty is how I learned to stand tall in the face of adversity. Surrendering to God's absolute supremacy is how I learned to major on the main things and not sweat small setbacks. Confessing that He's in total control of global weather and when the sun shines in my little corner of the world is how I learned to dance in the rain. Job 26 reveals that bowing before the bigness of God is what helped him navigate life better too.

> Read Psalm 110. What similarities do you find between this psalm and Job 26?
>
> They both indicate the great power of God. to make everything "right."

Read Acts 2:14-36. Why do you think Peter used Psalm 110 as proof that Jesus was the Messiah in his first sermon to an audience of religious Jews?

Read Mark 10:15-16. What do you think Jesus meant by saying we need to receive the kingdom of God like a little child?

We need the innocense + total faith of a child —

YOUR STORY

In John Calvin's seminal thesis about Christianity, *Institutes of the Christian Religion*, he penned this famous passage about how God has to condescend to communicate to us:

> For who even of slight intelligence does not understand that, as nurses commonly do with infants, God is wont in a measure to "lisp" in speaking to us? Thus such forms of speaking do not so much express clearly what God is like as accommodate the knowledge of him to our slight capacity. To do this he must descend far beneath his loftiness.[8]

What Calvin is asserting here is that our Creator and Redeemer has to "dumb Himself down" in order for us to understand Him. Does that make you feel special and cared for or embarrassed by your deficiency? Explain your answer.

Carve out at least fifteen minutes during the day and another fifteen minutes after the sun's gone down (or as my little girl says, "gone to sleep"), and lie on the ground in your yard or a public park and ponder the sky. Immediately afterwards write a short psalm of your own, extolling God's creative ability.

Using the following letters of the alphabet as a guide, list one of your favorite attributes/characteristics of God that begins with each of the twenty-six corresponding letters (i.e. **A**biding, **B**eckoning, **C**ompassionate …)

A *almighty*

B

C *caring*

D *devoted*

E

F *faithful*

G *grace-filled*

H

i

J

K

L

M

N

O

P

Q

R

S

T

U

V

W

X

Y

Z

Write your greatest heartache or hardship in the space below. (Feel free to use code words or abbreviations for privacy.) After reviewing the twenty-six attributes of God you listed previously, write three possible scenarios in which this problem could be redeemed into a praise. (Example: *Knowing God is faithful helps me trust Him even though we are struggling financially.*)

In your opinion, which of the scenarios you've listed above has the most likely redemptive outcome? Why? What are you doing practically to "reach out for the fringe of Jesus' robe" so as to receive healing in this situation?

LEGAL CONCEPTS IN THE BOOK OF JOB

BY HARRY D. CHAMPY, III

Have you ever felt completely helpless? My children used to worry about the drain in the bathtub. Watching the water spiral down, they worried that they might get sucked out of sight. Job must have felt the same way. He was innocent (1:1,8; 2:3), but he was suffering. In addition, his friends accused him of some hidden sin. The more Job maintained his innocence, the more his friends accused him.

Cycle after cycle, the argument continued. Job probably felt stuck and helpless. Frustrated, Job turned to God, the only One who could prove his innocence. To make his claim, Job appealed directly to God, expressed his trust with legal terms, and thoroughly presented his case in chapters 29–31.

JOB'S PRESENTATION OF HIS CASE

Appealing Directly to God—In English, "you" can be either singular or plural. However, in Hebrew, second person singular and plural verbs have different grammatical forms. In Job's dialogue, the use of these forms is illuminating: Job used the plural to speak to the friends as a group. In contrast, most of Job's singular verbs were direct appeals to God: 7:7-21; 9:28-31; 10:2-22; 13:20-28; 14:1-2; 16:6-8; and 17:3-4. Job's longest appeal was in 10:2-22. Job's frustration was evident: "Is it good for *You to oppress* [italics for second-person verbs, suffixes, and imperatives added for emphasis], *to reject* the work of *Your hands*, and *favor* the plans of the wicked?" (10:3, HCSB). God's care of Job in the past had turned to crushing. "Please *remember* that *You formed me* like clay. ... *You clothed me* with skin and flesh, and *wove me* together with bones and tendons. *You gave me* life and faithful love, and *Your care* has guarded my life" (vv. 9, 11-12, HCSB). "If I am proud, *You hunt me* like a lion and *again display Your miraculous power* against me. *You produce* new *witnesses* against me and *multiply Your anger* toward me. Hardships assault me, wave after wave" (vv. 16-17, HCSB).

Holding Out Hope—In spite of the dire condition of his circumstances, on occasion Job showed glimmers of hope. Readers can see that his trust progressed within the dialogue: (1) the need for a mediator who could pronounce a judgment that would be binding on God (9:32-35), (2) the desire for a temporary refuge and for God to call him forth after His anger had subsided (14:7-14), (3) the discovery of a heavenly witness who could argue his case with God (16:18-22), and (4) the revelation of a living Redeemer (19:23-27).

The first passage (9:32-35) was a lament with no hope. The second passage (14:7-14) contained a glimmer of hope as Job compared himself to the example of a tree; if a stump could show signs of life after the tree had been cut down, could God not offer hope to Job? The third passage (16:18-22) identified a potential source of help, a friend who would plead his case before God.

However, the fourth passage (19:23-27) was a confident proclamation of faith. Job declared that even if he died, he would still be able to see God because his Kinsman-Redeemer was alive and would redeem him. "But I know my living Redeemer, and He will stand on the dust at last. Even after my skin has been destroyed, yet I will see God in my flesh" (vv. 25-26, HCSB). Job's Redeemer would be revealed, and he would be restored. No earthly redeemer could enable Job to see God; Job was referring to a heavenly Redeemer—possibly God Himself!

Presenting Final Arguments—After the friends' arguments fell apart, Job gave the most thorough presentation of his case: Job remembered better days, his life with God (chap. 29); Job recounted the misery of the present, his life with suffering (chap. 30); and Job raised his voice in an oath of innocence, his life of integrity (chap. 31).

In the past, Job was right with God, and his blessed life proved it (29:2,14). Job even helped maintain justice, defending the poor, the fatherless, and the stranger (vv. 12,16).

In spite of his past, Job was suffering intensely. His physical pain was severe—with constant pain, restless nights, burning bones, and darkened skin (30:16-17,27-28,30). Worthless ones mocked him and spat in his face (vv. 1,9-10). To make his humiliation worse, Job could not find any help from God, the One actually attacking him (vv. 20-22).

Because he knew he was innocent, Job swore an oath of innocence (31:1). If he had done anything wrong, he would have deserved punishment, but he had not (v. 6). Job concluded his oath by affixing his signature and challenging God to present any evidence against him (v. 35).

JOB'S USE OF LEGAL TERMS OR ALLUSIONS

Job used many words that would cause the Hebrew reader to think of a legal setting—the equivalent of using words like "prosecute," "indictment," "plaintiff," or "attorney" today. Some of these words could be used outside of the courtroom, but the allusion to a courtroom is obvious. These terms can be placed into three broad categories: (1) words that are explicitly legal, (2) words that refer to a person's sin or guilt, and (3) ordinary words that can be used in a legal setting.

Words That Are Explicitly Legal—The words most explicitly connected with legal proceedings were the verbs *rib* ("contend," "argue a case," or "take someone to court"),[9] *yakach* ("argue," "argue a legal case," or "correct"), and *shaphatl* ("judge") and the nouns *tokechat* ("argument" or "case" from yakach) and *mishpatl* ("justice" or "judgment" from *shaphat*).

The verbal root *rib* developed in meaning from physical combat, to verbal combat, to legal proceedings. The word was primarily concerned with establishing who or what was right (*tsedeq*). The use of the word *rib* has come to identify a whole "lawsuit motif" or literary form in Job and the prophets. Some of the passages identified as lawsuit passages include Isaiah 3:12-15; Micah 6:1-8; Hosea 4:1-14; and the Book of Job.

Job felt as if he was being taken to court by his friends and God (10:2; 13:8,19; 23:6), and he wished he could take God to court (9:3). Elihu charged Job with taking God to court wrongly (33:13). Ironically, when God finally spoke out of the whirlwind, He asked Job if the one taking Him to court could really correct Him (40:2).

The verb *yakach* and its noun derivatives were primarily terms that referred to any aspect of the legal process: the accusation, a defendant's response, or even a witness. The participle *mokiach* can refer to one overseeing the process (a judge), a mediator, or any litigant.

Eliphaz first used this term: the man God corrected should be happy (5:17). Job had prepared his arguments (23:4) and wished that he could argue his case before God (9:3-35; 13:3,15; 23:7). Job desired an arbitrator who could argue or resolve his case (16:21). Elihu suggested that God used suffering to correct people (33:29-30). Job was looking for one who could argue his case, "not so much to impose a sentence as to settle a dispute while respecting justice."[10]

In a general sense, the decision of a trial was *mishpatl* ("justice"), and *shaphatl* was the act of judging. In a more technical sense, the words could refer to any process of government—legislative, executive, or judicial.

Bildad asked if God would pervert justice (8:3). Job knew that he was right (13:18), but God was depriving him of justice (19:7; 27:2). Job knew that God was the Heavenly Judge (9:15,24; 12:17; 21:22; 23:7), but God's justice had been so twisted that the wicked were protected (10:3). Job longed for deliverance from this type of justice (23:7).

Words That Refer to a Person's Sin or Guilt— Several Hebrew words refer to a person's sinning or not sinning: *tam* and *tummah* ("integrity"), the idea of being complete; *yashar* ("upright"), the idea of measuring up to a standard; *pesha'* ("transgression"), the breaching of a relationship; *'awon* ("iniquity"), the idea of being twisted; *chatta'ah* and *chatla* ("sin"), the idea of missing a mark or goal; *'awwal* ("wicked"), the idea of deviating from a standard; and *remiyah* ("deceit"). Job maintained that he was complete (31:6) and upright (23:7) and that he had not transgressed (31:33), committed iniquity (vv. 11,28), sinned (v. 30), acted wickedly (v. 3), or deceived (27:4). In a just legal system, sin would be equal to guilt.

Ordinary Words with Legal Implications— Numerous common Hebrew words can

Adapted from Harry D. Champy, III, "Legal Concepts in the Book of Job," *Biblical Illustrator*, Summer 2006, 54-58.

be used in a legal setting in addition to their normal uses. Examples include: 'abar ("to cross over"), darash ("to seek"), qara' ("to call"), 'anah ("to answer"), and qum ("to rise up").

The name "Hebrew" came from the verb 'abar because they had passed over the Jordan River. Job used the word both for overlooking sin (7:21) and punishing sin (13:13; 30:15).

Seeking or searching (darash) can, in some instances, sound like cross-examining (10:6). Likewise, summoning someone to court and responding to a legal accusation could be described with the ordinary words qara' (5:1; 9:16; 12:4; 13:22; 14:15; 19:16) and 'anah (9:3, 14-16,32; 12:4; 13:22; 14:15; 16:8; 23:5; 30:20; 31:35).

Job referred to evidence "rising up" (qum) against him (16:8), to his Redeemer who would stand (qum) to deliver him (19:25), and to God's standing up (qum) to punish (31:14).

THE VERDICT

In his pursuit of vindication, Job turned to God—using legal terminology. Job was well-acquainted with the legal process. He had sat in the gate and administered justice (29:7-17). As his friends were probably "colleagues," the book sounds like a conversation between lawyers or judges who naturally used forensic words to describe their ordinary experiences. This legal theme. then became the framework of the entire book.

Since God's covenant was basically a legal contract, the forensic nature of this book applied to every member of the covenant community. Likewise, it continues to apply to the church today, which means that we can learn lessons from Job's experiences.

Earthly justice, as Job's friends summarized, is imperfect because humans have limited knowledge and make generalizations. The friends did not know about God's judgment of Job's character (1:8; 2:3), and they generalized their own observations to Job's situation. These actions remind us that only God, not a human legal system, can justify and save.

Job took his claim directly to God and trusted in his heavenly Redeemer. Job's actions affirm that doubt and confusion should be taken directly to God, not necessarily to others. God spoke to Job from a whirlwind and bombarded him with numerous questions (38:1–41:34). Job's summons had been answered, and he was able to see and experience God in a new way (42:5). Knowing that God loved him enough to speak to him and that God was all-powerful, Job retracted his legal claim (v. 6). Job's demeanor and attitude completely changed. Rather than defensive and challenging, Job was now contented and contrite. We too can find our ultimate contentment in God.

And Job's "sentence"? "The Lord blessed the latter part of Job's life more than the earlier. ... Job lived 140 years after this and saw his children and their children to the fourth generation. Then Job died, old and full of days" (42:12,16-17, HCSB).

Shame is self-focused; bad things are
deserved; pulls us away fr God
It traps us.

Repentence: God focused; leads
to liberty & joy (we are aware of
our faults)

Job 32: 1-13 Elihu   Job 33: 1-33

33:16 "he uncovers their ears"
/God will get your attention thru Pain"

Psalm 119:75 ... you have afflicted
me fairly

- most pain can be used fr God's glory -
God's pain will makes us healthy

Job 33: 23-27 "his skin will be healthier"
Repentence - you say I messed up but
let me tell you about God
Holding in our sin makes us sick!

Video sessions available for purchase
or rent at www.LifeWay.com/Job

DISCUSSION QUESTIONS:

What one thing from the video teaching was new or interesting to you?

How would you define repentance?

How does repentance lead to joy? How have you experienced that in your life?

What's the difference between shame *and* repentance?

How does secret shame keep you trapped?

Has God ever gotten your attention through pain? Explain.

Lisa says that most pain can be used for God's purposes. Do you agree? Why or why not?

How would you explain rehabilitative pain? How have you seen God use rehabilitative pain for His purposes in your life?

5

A BETTER KIND OF WOUND CARE

READING ASSIGNMENT:

Read Job 32–37 between now and watching the next video teaching. Feel free to read the passage in sections (maybe one chapter at a time). If possible, try to read through this section of Scripture at least twice so that the meaning behind these words begins to sink in.

MY STORY

Choosing *not* to tell my parents about being abused by those men in a bar when I was a child set the course for how I dealt with pain for decades afterwards. By the time I was a teenager, I'd become very adept at smiling on the outside while dying on the inside. Unfortunately, keeping my "bad" and "sad" feelings locked up in a closet to which only I had the key gave those feelings time and space to grow and fester like emotional gangrene. Eventually my untended pain was powerful enough to impede my ability to have deep, healthy relationships. That's why I spent the better part of young adulthood subconsciously avoiding men who could love me well and was instead drawn to abusive or emotionally distant men. This also led me to develop codependent friendships with women. From my earliest years, I had a *legitimate* need to be held and healed, but because that need wasn't taken care of wholly and appropriately, I ended up self-medicating in *illegitimate* ways. I firmly believe that when we don't allow the Lord to lance our heart wounds, they get infected and make us sick. Furthermore, untended wounds can cause massive collateral damage because just one precious, yet septic soul has the potential to poison every person they rub shoulders with.

One of the most tragic biblical examples of this is found in the story of Tamar, King David's daughter.

Some time passed. David's son Absalom had a beautiful sister named Tamar, and David's son Amnon was infatuated with her. Amnon was frustrated to the point of making himself sick over his sister Tamar because she was a virgin, but it seemed impossible to do anything to her. Amnon had a friend named Jonadab, a son of David's brother Shimeah. Jonadab was a very shrewd man, and he asked Amnon, "Why are you, the king's son, so miserable every morning? Won't you tell me?"

Amnon replied, "I'm in love with Tamar, my brother Absalom's sister."

Jonadab said to him, "Lie down on your bed and pretend you're sick. When your father comes to see you, say to him, 'Please let my sister Tamar come and give me something to eat. Let her prepare a meal in my presence so I can watch and eat from her hand.'"

So Amnon lay down and pretended to be sick. When the king came to see him, Amnon said to him, "Please let my sister Tamar come and make a couple of cakes in my presence so I can eat from her hand."

David sent word to Tamar at the palace: "Please go to your brother Amnon's house and prepare a meal for him."

Then Tamar went to his house while Amnon was lying down. She took dough, kneaded it, made cakes in his presence, and baked them. She brought the pan and set it down in front of him, but he refused to eat. Amnon said, "Everyone leave me!" And everyone left him. "Bring the meal to the bedroom," Amnon told Tamar, "so I can eat from your hand." Tamar took the cakes she had made and went to her brother Amnon's bedroom. When she brought them to him to eat, he grabbed her and said, "Come sleep with me, my sister!"

"Don't, my brother!" she cried. "Don't disgrace me, for such a thing should never be done in Israel. Don't commit this outrage! Where could I ever go with my humiliation? And you—you would be like one of the outrageous fools in Israel! Please, speak to the king, for he won't keep me from you." But he refused to listen to her, and because he was stronger than she was, he disgraced her by raping her.

So Amnon hated Tamar with such intensity that the hatred he hated her with was greater than the love he had loved her with. "Get out of here!" he said.

"No," she cried, "sending me away is much worse than the great wrong you've already done to me!"

But he refused to listen to her. Instead, he called to the servant who waited on him: "Get this away from me, throw her out, and bolt the door behind her!" Amnon's servant threw her out and bolted the door behind her. Now Tamar was wearing a long-sleeved garment, because this is what the king's virgin daughters wore. Tamar put ashes on her head and tore the long-sleeved garment she was wearing. She put her hand on her head and went away crying out.

Her brother Absalom said to her: "Has your brother Amnon been with you? Be quiet for now, my sister. He is your brother. Don't take this thing to heart." So Tamar lived as a desolate woman in the house of her brother Absalom.

When King David heard about all these things, he was furious.

2 SAMUEL 13:1-21

Sadly, this true story proves that sexual abuse has been around since the beginning of time and so have the festering, untended wounds that all-too-often lie in its wake. In Tamar's case, not only does her own half-brother exploit her innocence to get her in a position where he can overpower and rape her, but after his heinous crime of passion, he adds to her agony by cruelly and publicly kicking her out of his house. This deals a deathblow to her future, because in that era, a single woman who lost her virginity had virtually no chance at a decent marriage proposal. So not only did Amnon greedily satisfy his lust with his sister's body, he also wiped his filthy hands on the fabric of her future, leaving it forever stained.

Unfortunately, Tamar's untenable situation doesn't get much better. It's possible that Absalom, her full-blooded brother, might have had an inkling about Amnon's evil intentions, evidenced by his question to her, "Has your brother Amnon been with you?" (v. 20). If that's the case, perhaps he could have alerted David or at least confronted Amnon. And while Absalom cares for Tamar in providing a place for her to live, he also shushes her and tells her not to make a big deal out of being violently raped and having her virginity, her dignity, and her future stolen and desecrated beyond repair.

The travesty of shaming victims of sexual abuse has been trumpeted in our news cycle lately. However, Absalom's horrible advice to his stricken sister verifies that shaming the wounded is not a new smokescreen. Neither is King David's silent refusal to deal with this horrific family tragedy. While verse 21 confirms his anger regarding his baby girl's attack, as far as we can tell from Scripture, he never disciplined Amnon nor spoke of their incestuous nightmare again. This shocking incident was part of the snowball of tragic events that would fulfill Nathan's prophecy about the consequences of David's sin with Bathsheba (2 Sam. 12:11-15). Perhaps the widespread collateral damage would have been lessened if this royal family had not left the serious emotional wounds untreated. Instead, the following havoc reigned:

- Absalom murders his brother Amnon to avenge Tamar (2 Sam. 13:24-29).

- Instead of honoring his father, King David, and waiting for the possibility of his own coronation, Absalom betrays David and stages a coup (2 Sam. 15:1-14).

- Instead of having a consolidated military force that unilaterally protects Israel, the army's loyalty becomes divided between David and Absalom and, as a result, twenty thousand soldiers needlessly lose their lives (2 Sam. 18:7).

- Instead of succeeding his father, David, as the third king of Israel or serving as wise counsel to his brother and eventual king, Solomon, Absalom dies young and in a humiliating fashion (2 Sam. 18:9-15).

- Instead of enjoying the honor and protection they were accustomed to, ten more Israelite women are publicly raped and abused (2 Sam. 15:16; 16:22).

Although Job's story doesn't include the specific trauma of sexual abuse, it too serves as a case study for pain management. A living illustration, proving that allowing God to lance our wounds wards off infection, paves the way for miraculous healing, and even leads to better community health.

The word "desolate" used to describe Tamar's life after she was raped and shamed into silent resignation comes from the Hebrew word *shamem*, which means a state of ruin or destruction.

What kind of ruin (i.e. a strained relationship, a lack of trust, etc.) has resulted from unresolved pain or conflict in your past? How have you effectively treated that old emotional wound so that it doesn't become infected again?

Read Proverbs 24:11-12. How would you describe the relationship between shame and silence? How would you encourage an introvert or naturally shy person to express pain so that his or her wound doesn't become infected?

Read Ephesians 5:6-14. How would you explain this passage of Scripture to a child? How about to an adult who hasn't yet put his or her hope in Jesus Christ?

After the Week 5 video teaching taping for the *Job* Bible study, I had some people wanting more clarity about shame and repentance, especially as it related to the man of the hour. It seems I came across as subtly aligning with Elihu's encouragement for Job to repent. If true, that would be off-base in light of the text's ongoing affirmation of Job's innocence and his own insistence that he'd done nothing to deserve the calamity that had befallen him.

Just to be clear, unlike Eliphaz, Bildad, and Zophar, I don't *remotely* agree with their judgmental rationale that Job needed to repent for some hidden behavior that somehow caused the death and destruction he was facing! However, as fallible human beings whose hearts are deceitful apart from God's indwelling Holy Spirit (Jer. 17:9), I think it behooves *all of us* to live in an open-handed, tenderhearted posture of unpretentiousness before our Creator and Redeemer wherein we're in a perpetual state of asking Him:

> Search me, God, and know my heart;
> test me and know my concerns.
> See if there is any offensive way in me;
> lead me in the everlasting way.

> PSALM 139:23-24

I bear a striking resemblance to Paul's self-portrait:

> What I don't understand about myself is that I decide one way, but then I act another, doing things I absolutely despise.

> ROMANS 7:15, *THE MESSAGE*

So for me, repentance isn't just the singular act of confessing that I did something ungodly and need my heavenly Father's forgiveness for a specific sin. It's the continual awareness that I will always do ungodly things without His guidance, correction, and the transformative power of the Holy Spirit. It's my uninterrupted plea for sanctification. It's my moment-by-moment spiritual *mea culpa*. It's the life rope I've attached to God's holiness so I won't drift away from the awesome destiny He's designed especially for me. It's the position of humility that keeps me happily secure under His protective wings. It's the daily, proverbial Post-It® note reminding me that only God is the sovereign ruler of the universe, and He doesn't need my input. It's my road to personal revival, as well as, I believe, the only route to corporate revival (2 Chron. 7:14). And for me, repentance doesn't always express itself in head-bowed, red-faced penance before Jesus. In fact, more often than not, it's expressed with a head-bobbing, happy dance because I'm so overjoyed by the intimacy repentance affords me with the King of all kings!

Which was surely the kind of spiritual payoff Elihu was preaching about in Job 36 when he connected the dots between repentance and restorative happiness:

> If people are bound with chains
> and trapped by the cords of affliction,
> God tells them what they have done
> and how arrogantly they have transgressed.
> *He opens their ears to correction*
> *and tells them to repent from iniquity.*
> *If they listen and serve him,*
> *they will end their days in prosperity*
> *and their years in happiness.*
> But if they do not listen,
> they will cross the river of death
> and die without knowledge.
>
> Those who have a godless heart harbor anger;
> even when God binds them, they do not cry for help.
> They die in their youth;
> their life ends among male cult prostitutes.
> God rescues the afflicted by their affliction;
> he instructs them by their torment.
>
> Indeed, he lured you from the jaws of distress
> to a spacious and unconfined place.
> Your table was spread with choice food.
>
> JOB 36:8-16, *EMPHASIS MINE*

Can you remember a season when God instructed you in your torment? Explain.

Do you agree with this famous C. S. Lewis quote in that same vein: "Pain insists upon being attended to. God whispers to us in our pleasures, speaks in our conscience, but shouts in our pains: it is His megaphone to rouse a deaf world"[1]? Why or why not?

Read Proverbs 29:1. How would you synopsize this verse into a no-more-than-five-words book or movie title? How would you compose a proverb to express the exact opposite of this one?

How would you describe your personal posture of tenderhearted humility when it comes to interacting with the Creator of the universe?

KEY POINTS TO PONDER IN JOB'S STORY

Tamar's story illustrates how shame can lead to isolation and possible widespread destruction. However, this section of Job's story carries the promise that *repentance leads to restoration* and likely much more prolific fruit than was produced before being pruned. We'll see this actually come true in the epilogue of this book. While the third common response to pain and hardship woven throughout this Old Testament narrative is *guilt*—the feeling of responsibility or remorse for an offense, crime, or wrong whether real or imagined.

When I was a young woman, newly commissioned in vocational ministry, I visited a friend's church multiple times to glean wisdom from her pastor, who was both a brilliant theologian and fiery orator. I took such fast, copious notes when listening to him preach that I'd usually have to vigorously shake my writing hand halfway through the service to keep it from cramping up. My own theological scaffolding was pretty dinky in those early, pre-seminary days, so I couldn't hold on to half of what he was expounding, much less recognize any doctrinal flaws. However, I did feel uneasy every time he went on a rampage about sexual sins. The more he yelled about the "wicked fornicators" of our generation, the more the veins in his neck would bulge and his face would turn beet red. I remember thinking, *Somebody better have 911 on hold, because I think he's about to have a heart attack.* I can also remember exactly where I was when I got the news that he'd been caught propositioning male prostitutes and had massive files of pornography on his church computer.

Much like untended emotional wounds get infected and make us heart sick, unprocessed guilt hardens into an angry knot that causes us to wallop innocent bystanders with an accusatory smack. It's basically the pot calling the kettle black kind of hypocrisy. Or, as Shakespeare poetically framed contrived innocence in *Hamlet*, "The lady doth protest too much, methinks"[2]—which could very well have been written about Job's three prideful friends, Eliphaz, Bildad, and Zophar. They've been quick to point blaming fingers at him but refuse to admit any spiritual culpability of their own. Their stiff self-righteousness stands in stark contrast with Job's pliant heart that's palpable even before he "officially" repents in the last few chapters of this story. In fact, look at how tender his heart is toward the poor and the powerless in Job 31:

> Have I ever been unfair to my employees
> when they brought a complaint to me?
> What, then, will I do when God confronts me?
> When God examines my books, what can I say?

Didn't the same God who made me, make them?
Aren't we all made of the same stuff, equals before God?

Have I ignored the needs of the poor,
turned my back on the indigent,
Taken care of my own needs and fed my own face
while they languished?
Wasn't my home always open to them?
Weren't they always welcome at my table?

Have I ever left a poor family shivering in the cold
when they had no warm clothes?
Didn't the poor bless me when they saw me coming,
knowing I'd brought coats from my closet?

If I've ever used my strength and influence
to take advantage of the unfortunate,
Go ahead, break both my arms,
cut off all my fingers!
The fear of God has kept me from these things—
how else could I ever face him?

JOB 31:13-23, *THE MESSAGE*

Whether the genesis of the pain and hardship you've had to walk through was caused through no fault of your own, like Job's agony, was the consequence of bad, perhaps even sinful, decisions, or was the result of God's sovereign, albeit mysterious pruning, we all have a choice in how we respond after we've been injured. We can choose to isolate in shame, become prickly and accusatory because of guilt, or move toward God in the tenderhearted posture of humility, trust, and repentance—the only path to healing and restoration.

Read again Job 33:19-30. Eliphaz, Bildad, and Zophar viewed Job's suffering as punishment from God for sin, whereas Elihu views it as corrective discipline. How would you describe the difference between the two views?

Read 1 Corinthians 11:32. What does Paul's message to the believers in Corinth have in common with young Elihu's message to Job?

Read Luke 22:31. How did Peter's initial response to Satan's sifting (Luke 22:54-62) differ from Job's initial response to Satan's sifting (Job 1:3-22)? And how are the latter chapters of these two men's post-sifting stories similar (Job 42; John 21:1-19)?

KEY CHARACTER IN JOB'S STORY

OK, I know it's probably no surprise that Elihu is the key character for this week, and not simply because he's the *only* character besides Job in this section of dialogue. I've also come to think of him as a little brother of sorts. I mean, with six entire chapters devoted to his monologue, he's obviously prone to verbosity, so there's that family resemblance. Then there's his penchant for bombastic rhetoric, and my sister will gladly tell you with rolled eyes that I developed this irritating trait soon after exiting the womb. Finally, there's his deep fondness for the Holy Spirit, which totally resonates with my bouncy Bapticostal self.

Seriously though, Elihu refers to "the spirit" three times in the first twenty verses of his opening speech. There is some debate on whether or not he is speaking of the Holy Spirit.[3] But he does describe "the spirit" (or "Spirit") as the "breath" of God:

> But it is the spirit in a person—
> the breath from the Almighty—
> that gives anyone understanding.

JOB 32:8

> The Spirit of God has made me,
> and the breath of the Almighty gives me life.

JOB 33:4

The Hebrew word for *spirit* is *ruwach*, an onomatopoeic term that sounds like an exhalation. It is used throughout the Old Testament to speak of the Spirit of God, including Genesis 1:2. While Elihu may not have understood the concept of the Trinity as we do, he did understand that the power of God was at work in him, giving life and wisdom.

Elihu's charismatic leanings are also exposed in the way he emphasizes God communicating with His people through dreams and visions:

> For God speaks time and again,
> but a person may not notice it.
> In a dream, a vision in the night,

when deep sleep comes over people
as they slumber on their beds.

JOB 33:14-15

As well as in his demonstrative, uninhibited tone:

My heart pounds at this
and leaps from my chest.
Just listen to his thunderous voice
and the rumbling that comes from his mouth.
He lets it loose beneath the entire sky;
his lightning to the ends of the earth.

Then there comes a roaring sound;
God thunders with his majestic voice.
He does not restrain the lightning
when his rumbling voice is heard.
God thunders wondrously with his voice;
he does great things that we cannot comprehend.

JOB 37:1-5

It's easy to imagine Elihu's voice rising in pitch and his arms waving dramatically while he enthusiastically describes the majesty of God to Job. Perhaps this was a breath of fresh air to Job, lifting him up out of the gutter where his three sanctimonious friends had left him.

Are you one to speak of God with exuberance and enthusiasm? Explain. Why does the way we speak of God to others matter so much?

Read Job 32:18-19 and Matthew 9:17. Why do you think both Elihu and Jesus used wineskins as a metaphor for spiritual renewal?

Despite Elihu's pretentious, wind-baggy ways, he was used much like John the Baptist to prepare the way for God. How has God used an unlikely, perhaps even irritating, person in your life to pave the way for spiritual renewal?

YOUR STORY

Spend some time sifting through the layers of your heart to ascertain three wounds that aren't yet completely healed. Some of these wounds may be traumatic incidents from childhood that are scarred over and buried so deeply you rarely excavate them anymore. Others might be relatively fresh injuries that, when poked, have the power to leave you reeling in emotional pain. List all three wounds in the space below. (Feel free to abbreviate or code these three descriptions for the sake of privacy.)

1.

2.

3.

Now prayerfully consider whether any shame or guilt is still attached to any of these heartaches. If so, write the corresponding letter **S** for shame or **G** for guilt next to that specific wound.

Next, speak Psalm 139:23-24 over each injury. Ask God if there's anything you need to repent of or anyone from whom you need to ask forgiveness. If He reveals a need for confession and repentance and/or prompts you to perform an act of forgiveness, take whatever time you need to respond humbly and thoroughly. This might involve seeking pastoral care, Christian counseling, or arranging to meet an old foe for coffee. It may simply be spending some time on your knees in contrition before our Redeemer who "is a compassionate and gracious God, slow to anger and abounding in faithful love and truth" (Ex. 34:6).

Once the Holy Spirit confirms in your heart and mind that each wound has been properly cared for and will heal in a way that glorifies God and will be good for you, cover the **S** or **G** with a big red **R** for restoration. If you don't mind a messy study guide, you might want to cut out the written "wounds" with scissors and burn those scraps of paper, to symbolize that those old wounds have finally been spiritually cauterized and don't have the power to inflict any more damage in your life.

If, in your search through your heart, you joyfully find no lingering wounds, old or fresh, take a moment to thank the Lord for His healing in your life. Then consider those around you who you know are still dealing with deep hurts. Spend time praying that they would also find healing and freedom in Christ, and make yourself available to the Lord to be a help and support in their restoration.

ELIHU: JOB'S FOURTH FRIEND

BY R. RAYMOND LLOYD

Job stood on the oath of his innocence. He cried out for the Almighty to answer him (31:35). His three friends, Eliphaz, Bildad, and Zophar, were now silent. They failed to convince Job of his sins. Suddenly bursting upon the scene with great gusto and emotion is Elihu,[4] young, articulate, arrogant, passionate, and claiming to have divine wisdom and to be a mediator in the dispute between Job and God.

Who was this brash youth? More fully identified than Job's other friends, Elihu, meaning "he is my God," is introduced by both father and family. His father was Barachel, the Buzite, not mentioned elsewhere in the Old Testament. The name means "blessed of God." Along with his own name, this perhaps is an indication of Elihu's spiritual heritage.

Buz was Abraham's nephew (Gen. 22:21-23) probably indicating Aramean roots.[5] As a member of the family of Ram, he had ancestral ties to the tribe of Judah (Ruth 4:19; 1 Chron. 2:9-12). The spiritual heritage and Aramean and Judean linkage are unique factors that distinguish Elihu from Job's other friends,[6] whom the text introduced simply by tribal affiliation.

In the five verses of prose introduction to the poetic speeches (Job 32:1-5), Elihu's basic attitude is clearly presented. He was an angry young man who had listened to the preceding debate and waited impatiently for his turn to speak.

Four times he is described as "angry." He was angry with Job "because he justified himself rather than God" (v. 2, HCSB) and with the three friends for their bungling inability to refute Job (v. 3).

Elihu then delivered a rather long "apology" for his further speeches. With respect for age, he had waited to speak. He now characterized himself as "timid" and "afraid"—certainly not reflected in his speeches. He claimed that wisdom is not necessarily a gift of age (vv. 7-9) but is from the "spirit in man and the breath of the Almighty" that gives "him understanding" (v. 8, HCSB). This is in contrast to the three friends who based their claims on tradition. Elihu claimed inspiration by the Spirit of God gave him insight that may be trusted despite his youth. Here the purpose of Elihu's presence in the plot of the book is at least partly clarified, namely, that his words were offered under the claim of divine inspiration. Job on several occasions sought for an arbiter in his case with God

(9:33; 16:21; 31:35).[7] As his friends were speechless, Elihu grasped the opportunity to be the new spokesman for the defense and shed some new light on the subject. The stage was now set for Elihu's four discourses on God's nature. His thesis was twofold: God disciplines persons to turn them from their erroneous ways, and God with complete impartiality governs justly and with awesome power rules sovereignly.[8]

FIRST DISCOURSE, THE IMMANENCE OF GOD (JOB 33)

Job had contended that God had not answered his claims (vv. 12-13). Elihu assured Job that God had indeed spoken. Job evidently had missed it, though: "For God speaks time and again, but a person may not notice it" (v. 14, HCSB). Elihu, in his first discourse, instructed that God did intimately communicate with humankind in a variety of ways: through dreams, through suffering, and through a mediator.

The purpose for this communication was so He could ultimately redeem and deliver the individual (vv. 15-30).

SECOND DISCOURSE, THE OMNIPOTENCE AND OMNISCIENCE OF GOD (JOB 34)

Job claimed that he was innocent and that God was unjust (vv. 5-6). Here Elihu refuted Job's claim in much the same manner as his three friends. However, he was more concerned with presenting an omnipotent and omniscient God (vv. 21-30) of justice, who plays no favorites, than attempting to prove Job was in the wrong.

THIRD DISCOURSE, THE TRANSCENDENCE OF GOD (JOB 35)

Job claimed to be more righteous than God (v. 2, KJV). Elihu reminded Job that God is independent and cannot be controlled by man's actions (vv. 1-8). God's nature cannot be affected by the activity, good or bad, of the individual. Yet Elihu stated that man is to seek after God, not so much for what He can do for us, but simply because He is God (vv. 9-12). Human beings want God's help but fail to believe God is good and to trust Him as the Creator of life, who provides "songs in the night" (v. 10). Old Testament scholar Samuel Terrien gives a fitting summary to this whole thought: "There is also in pain and grief a constructive potentiality: if man knows the higher purpose of the Creator, he ought to endure injury better than the mass of a bleeding humanity among whom 'None saith, Where is God my maker who giveth songs in the night?' (v. 10)."[9]

FOURTH DISCOURSE, THE MYSTERY AND MAJESTY OF GOD (JOB 36–37)

In a much more compassionate tone and in a fervent expression of praise, Elihu elaborated on the mystery of God's disciplinary use of suffering. God seeks to open a person's ears through tribulations, that they may turn to obey and serve Him (36:5-15). Following one final warning to

Job to cease his accusation of God, Elihu focused on the majesty and glory of God that surpasses all human understanding, as revealed in nature (36:26–37:13). Some interpreters of the book view the speeches of Elihu as contributing nothing new to the plot of the story. Some would suggest Elihu's contribution is a secondary insertion in the book and that Job's final speech calling for the Almighty to answer him (31:35) was originally followed by Yahweh's response beginning in chapter 38.[10]

The Elihu portion of the book makes several unique and distinct contributions to the book. It thus serves as a vital part of the whole dramatic story.

1. Elihu claimed to speak under the inspiration of the Spirit.

2. Elihu did not assume, as did Job's other three friends, that all suffering is a direct consequence of past sin. Instead, he strongly affirmed that God uses dreams and sufferings themselves to awaken a man's conscience in order to keep him from a wrong course. Elihu appears to have come into the story at this point specifically to bring a new and unique thought to the mystery of suffering, going beyond the traditional belief that suffering is punishment to the revolutionary idea that it may well be disciplinary.

3. Elihu encouraged Job to focus on God's transcendent characteristics— His splendor and His power. He also encouraged Job to respond wisely, not by engaging in dispute with God, but instead to humbly submit in fear to God. This is a major thrust of the wisdom writer: "The fear of the LORD—that is wisdom" (28:28, HCSB).

4. Job called out for the Almighty to answer him. Now Elihu, having been sent, prepared the way for the Voice in the whirlwind in much the same manner as John the Baptist was the forerunner of the Messiah in the New Testament. The final act of the drama is ready to unfold. The way was prepared.

Through cycles of debate, Job defended and upheld his innocence. Elihu, along with Job's other three friends, had ridiculed, criticized, and accused Job. Now, though, all four friends stood silent and in awe. The climactic theophany was about to begin. Yahweh was ready to speak to Job.

Adapted from R. Raymond Lloyd, "Elihu: Job's Fourth Friend," *Biblical Illustrator*, Summer 2006, 68-71.

Video sessions available for purchase
or rent at www.LifeWay.com/Job

DISCUSSION QUESTIONS:

What one thing from the video teaching was new or interesting to you?

Lisa says that how you respond to pain makes you either bitter or better. What does she mean? How have you experienced both?

Do you believe that God is present with you in your pain? Regardless of what kind of pain or how deep the pain goes? Explain.

How have you experienced God's presence in your pain? How has His presence led to unlikely joy?

Have you ever experienced a time when you went before God and realized you were doing all the talking and needed to stop and listen? Explain.

How are you doing at listening to God? What might be blocking your ability to hear Him?

Why is it that we spend more time wanting answers from God, rather than just wanting Him?

How has God carried you through your most difficult times?

Are you able to say in the painful situations that you are facing, "Lord, now that I've seen You, that is enough"? Why or why not?

6

SEEING YOU SETTLES ME

READING ASSIGNMENT:

Read Job 38:1–42:6 between now and watching the next video teaching. Read through the passage at least twice so that the meaning behind these words begins to sink in.

MY STORY

Toward the latter part of our adoption journey I was forced to move Missy to an orphanage. Haiti's adoption laws were changing, and it was very likely that I would lose her if I kept her in her home village instead of complying with the government mandate to transition her to an accredited facility. I flew down to stay with her during the first week of transition, which was even more agonizing than I expected. She was traumatized from being quite literally pulled from the embrace of her great aunt Fifi—who'd been taking care of her since her first mama, Marie, died—and driven away from the only home she'd ever known. She went from her rural village to a big orphanage surrounded by walls and razor wire in a strange city on a mountain two hours away.

My adoption agent, Christian counselor, and several adoption advocates strongly encouraged me *not* to make the trip with her from Neply, her village, to Pétion-Ville, where the orphanage was located. They explained that if I did she'd associate me with the shocking heartbreak of being torn from everyone and everything she knew. But, they explained, if I was waiting at the orphanage when she got there, then she'd view me as her safe place since I'd be the only familiar face at the facility. (By that time I'd visited her village multiple times, and she was already calling me *Mama Blan*, which means "White Mama.") They were probably right. But I will never forget the sheer terror on her precious little face when they first brought her to me in the guest house (a modest dorm-like building above the orphanage where would-be adoptive parents stayed). I thought, *If it's at all possible for me to be by my daughter's side when she's facing something really scary in the future, I will not allow her to endure something like this alone again.*

The moment I reached for her, she hurled herself into my arms, buried her face in my neck, and began to sob uncontrollably. And that's how she stayed all night long. She clung to me in our little twin bed in that oppressively hot, cinder block room with fickle electricity and just wailed, utterly inconsolable. I couldn't get her to eat anything the following morning, so I just walked up and down the steps beside the orphanage over and over again with Missy on my hip. She refused to speak or be set down. (This particular orphanage is located in a high-crime area, so armed guards are posted at the high metal entry gates and no one is allowed to venture outside on their own.) I kept trying to pique her interest in the more than sixty kids in the orphanage below the guest house, whom we could hear reciting their school lessons or noisily playing tag at recess. But anytime I walked her near the fence where she could see them, she shook her head violently and arched her back trying to get as far away from them as possible. I could only understand bits and pieces of what Missy said the few times she did speak that week because my Creole is very limited. However, she made it crystal clear that she was not an orphan like all those other kids because even though her Mama Marie had died she still had her Auntie and her Grandmama. Then she'd fix her big brown eyes on me with a serious expression, point her little finger at me, and proclaim, *Ou Mama Blan*— as if to say, *You are my mama now, and you better not leave me in this dreadful place.*

I didn't sleep one wink the last night of her first week in the orphanage, knowing that I had to leave Missy the next day and return to Nashville to continue the legal wrangling to get her home. I just held my now sleeping daughter on my chest and begged God to protect her heart and mind. I realized that for the first time in her four years, she'd be completely alone, without anyone to hold her, sing her to sleep, or advocate for her health. My heart hurt so badly that night, it was literally a physical ache in my chest. It became almost unbearable the next morning when one of the nannies from the orphanage appeared at breakfast. The director explained that the nanny had come to take Missy since the driver was ready to take me to the airport.

Of course Missy began to shriek and, as if she were a panicked octopus, wrapped her arms and legs around me as tightly as she could. All I wanted to do was carry her to the airport with me and take her home. But since our adoption wasn't finalized yet, we wouldn't make it past the ticket counter in Port-au-Prince, much less to Miami. Instead, I told the director that I would be walking Missy down to the orphanage myself, not handing her over to a nanny she didn't know. He frowned because they don't normally allow prospective parents to go down to the orphanage. However, when he realized I wasn't going to budge, he sighed and waved his hand dismissively while the nanny glared at me for a long moment, and then turned around in a huff, motioning for me to follow her.

There are five flights of cement stairs on the other side of a locked gate that you have to climb down to get to the orphanage from the guest house. The further we descended the louder Missy protested, "No, Mama, no! I lub you, Mama Blan! Souple (please), *Mama, no!*" When we got to the small, dank room she'd be sharing with twenty or so other children, the exasperated nanny gestured roughly to Missy's "bed," which was more like a dog kennel. It was completely enclosed with metal bars and had a door with a sliding lock on the outside. Since their organization only had three or four nannies to supervise more than sixty children, the beds they used for the smallest kids were essentially cages that prevented them from getting out at night. The director explained that they were for the children's safety, but I couldn't get past the claustrophobic cruelty of it, not to mention the cacophony of that many children crammed in a small building, most of whom were clamoring for attention or something to eat.

The entire time I was trying to get Missy settled in and settled down, there were five or six pitiful punkins pulling at my legs and grabbing frantically for the supplies I'd brought for her (clothes, a soft blanket, etc.). This only served to increase my daughter's anxiety. In the melee of the nanny sternly trying to usher me out of the room and other children screaming and crying, I put my hands gently on either side of Missy's tear-stained face and forced her to look at me. Then I calmly told her that I loved her with all my heart and that I would come back for her. Then I emphasized how Jesus/*Jezi* loved her even more than I did, and He would never, ever leave her.

The most difficult thing I've ever had to do in my life was turn away from my precious, panicked child and trudge back up those cement steps while she screamed, "*Mama! Mama! Mwen regret sa* (I'm sorry)! *Mama! Mwen regret sa se konsa* (I'm so sorry)!" She was only four years old. She had no idea that I had to go back to America to keep pushing the adoption ball up an almost impossibly steep Haitian hill if there was any chance for our adoption to be finalized. So she assumed she must've done something wrong and that's why I was leaving. Because I struggled with crippling shame for so many years over my own childhood traumas, it was almost more than I could bear. I could still hear her screaming she was sorry when I got up to the guest house. The driver hustled me out to the car so I wouldn't miss my flight. That's when I finally let myself break down. I sobbed over the necessary but terrible treason of abandoning my baby girl to a cage in a dirty, overcrowded orphanage with an angry caregiver.

I had two failed adoption attempts prior to Missy, buried both of my fathers, and lost several dear friends. But *nothing* in my life has eviscerated my soul like leaving Missy to fend for herself on that terrible summer day in June 2013. I died a thousand deaths over the next nine months because of the glacial pace and lackadaisical manner of the agencies who were handling the details of our adoption. My heart was broken by the fact that most of the nannies at the orphanage refused to touch Missy, much less pick her up, because they were afraid they'd get HIV through any physical contact. So she was shunned and kept mostly to herself. As I shared in the last teaching video, things got so bad that at one point I was told our adoption wasn't going to be finalized after all, and it looked like I was going to have to move to Haiti or lose her.

Thankfully, by the grace of God—who *still* parts Red Seas—I finally got to bring Missy home on April 14, 2014. Let me tell you, the last night we spent in that Haitian guest house, huddled together once again on a thin twin mattress in a hot, sticky room with no electricity and only a trickle of cold water in the bare-bones bathroom was *dramatically* different than the other sleepless nights we'd shared together there. Instead of insomnia brought on by dread and deep concerns, I couldn't sleep because I was so excited. I grinned so big for so long while tracing the outline of my sleeping daughter's face, my cheeks began to cramp. Then, when she began to snore, I laughed out loud. *She's coming home! She's coming home! My snoring angel is coming home!*

The emotions I had on April 13, 2014, weren't just as different as night and day compared to the other nights I'd spent with Missy in Haiti. They were as radically contrasting as the absolute darkness of a deep cavern to the brilliant glare of the high-noon sun in the desert. That extreme swing from rupture to rapture is similar to the dramatic shift that occurs in Job's journey. He goes from horrible loss at the beginning to happy contentment at the end. Who would've thought such awful torment could lead to such absolute joy? Some might even call it unlikely. *(Sorry, I just had to!)*

> Have you ever had an experience you'd describe as raw agony?
> If so, when and why?

What's your personal example of a "rupture to rapture" season?

Have you ever felt completely abandoned by someone else? If so, how did you deal with it? Have you ever felt completely abandoned by God? If so, how did you deal with it?

Job's raw agony was evidenced in many of the questions and complaints he posed to God. For instance:

> Why did you bring me out of the womb?
> I should've died and never been seen.
> JOB 10:18

> Why do you hide your face
> and consider me your enemy?
> JOB 13:24

> God hands me over to the unjust;
> he throws me to the wicked.
> I was at ease, but he shattered me;
> he seized me by the scruff of the neck
> and smashed me to pieces.
> JOB 16:11-12a

> He has made me an object of scorn to the people;
> I have become a man people spit at.
> JOB 17:6

But then God motions for a host of angels to take over His control panel for one hundred billion, *trillion* stars, swaggers to the edge of glory, and lassoes a hurricane to use as a megaphone:

> And now, finally, GOD answered Job from the eye of a violent storm.
> He said:

> Why do you confuse the issue?
> Why do you talk without knowing what you're talking about?
> Pull yourself together, Job!
> Up on your feet! Stand tall!
> I have some questions for you,
> and I want some straight answers.
> Where were you when I created the earth?
> Tell me, since you know so much!

Who decided on its size? Certainly you'll know that!
Who came up with the blueprints and measurements?
How was its foundation poured,
and who set the cornerstone,
While the morning stars sang in chorus
and all the angels shouted praise?
And who took charge of the ocean
when it gushed forth like a baby from the womb?
That was me! I wrapped it in soft clouds,
and tucked it in safely at night.
Then I made a playpen for it,
a strong playpen so it couldn't run loose,
And said, "Stay here, this is your place.
Your wild tantrums are confined to this place."

And have you ever ordered Morning, "Get up!"
told Dawn, "Get to work!"
So you could seize Earth like a blanket
and shake out the wicked like cockroaches?
As the sun brings everything to light,
brings out all the colors and shapes,
The cover of darkness is snatched from the wicked—
they're caught in the very act!

Have you ever gotten to the true bottom of things,
explored the labyrinthine caves of deep ocean?
Do you know the first thing about death?
Do you have one clue regarding death's dark mysteries?
And do you have any idea how large this earth is?
Speak up if you have even the beginning of an answer.

Do you know where Light comes from
and where Darkness lives
So you can take them by the hand
and lead them home when they get lost?
Why, of course you know that.
You've known them all your life,
grown up in the same neighborhood with them!

Have you ever traveled to where snow is made,
seen the vault where hail is stockpiled,
The arsenals of hail and snow that I keep in readiness
for times of trouble and battle and war?
Can you find your way to where lightning is launched,
or to the place from which the wind blows?
Who do you suppose carves canyons
for the downpours of rain, and charts
the route of thunderstorms
That bring water to unvisited fields,
deserts no one ever lays eyes on,
Drenching the useless wastelands
so they're carpeted with wildflowers and grass?
And who do you think is the father of rain and dew,
the mother of ice and frost?
You don't for a minute imagine
these marvels of weather just happen, do you?

Can you catch the eye of the beautiful Pleiades sisters,
or distract Orion from his hunt?
Can you get Venus to look your way,
or get the Great Bear and her cubs to come out and play?
Do you know the first thing about the sky's constellations
and how they affect things on Earth?

Can you get the attention of the clouds,
and commission a shower of rain?
Can you take charge of the lightning bolts
and have them report to you for orders?

Who do you think gave weather-wisdom to the ibis,
and storm-savvy to the rooster?
Does anyone know enough to number all the clouds
or tip over the rain barrels of heaven
When the earth is cracked and dry,
the ground baked hard as a brick?

Can you teach the lioness to stalk her prey
and satisfy the appetite of her cubs

As they crouch in their den,
waiting hungrily in their cave?
And who sets out food for the ravens
when their young cry to God,
fluttering about because they have no food?

JOB 38, *THE MESSAGE*

Yikes, I almost feel sorry for Job, don't you? And I can totally picture his deer in the headlights expression, especially since I *caused* one of those recently. Here's the deal, it probably won't surprise you that I'm a bit of a mama bear when it comes to Missy. And when someone threatens my cub, well, I sometimes overreact a teensy bit (hard to believe, right?)—especially when it comes to Missy's medical condition.

Even though HIV has been diagnosed since the early eighties, there's still a lot of misinformation and fear surrounding it. I often find myself explaining that while Missy has HIV, by the grace of God and excellent medical care, the virus is completely undetectable in her bloodstream. (She hasn't registered positive on the most sensitive test for HIV that measures a mere twenty units of the virus in one million units of blood for more than four years.) It's much like being in remission, if you have cancer. Unfortunately, sometimes even after I've gently clarified what it means that Missy is utterly undetectable, ignorant questions like, "But what if another child eats off her plate?" or "Is it OK for her to swim in the same pool as 'normal' kids?" are still posed. At which moment I pause to say a quick prayer, and then I take a deep breath to make sure my tone is non-combative and my expression is friendly. And I remind myself that punching rude adults is rarely a good idea. Then I launch into a graphic, detailed explanation regarding how the virus is most commonly transmitted, which involves explicitly intimate and colorful—albeit medically correct—terminology. And I have to confess that I have rather enjoyed watching people's eyes widen and faces redden during my enlightening speech. A few times when talking with a particularly combative ignoramus about Missy being included in a communal activity (such as a gymnastics class or a team sport), I've even upped the ante by making eye contact with said prejudiced person for a long moment and then calmly but firmly proclaiming, "Oh and lastly, there's IV drug use—for instance when people shoot heroin with shared, dirty needles. But since I don't think any of those risky activities are permitted here on your watch and since there's *never* been a reported incident of HIV being transmitted through casual contact such as sharing lunch, a kiss, or even sitting on the same toilet seat *anywhere in the world*, there's really no chance that my daughter's illness could be considered contagious in this environment. As a matter of fact, statistically speaking, it's more likely that someone will be eaten by a great white shark here in land-locked Tennessee than 'catch' HIV from my kid."

I've even offered to lead a special parents' meeting where I provide this information for everyone in the program. Needless to say, I haven't been taken up on that offer yet. I get tickled thinking about all the stunned expressions I've caused in my personal eradicate-the-stigma-of-pediatric-HIV campaign. And it makes me wonder if God grinned when Job—who mere moments before had been stomping around, waving his fist at heaven and demanding an audience with Him—was basically stunned into submission. I can totally imagine poor Job's wide eyes and red face when he responded ever so meekly after God "explained" the real deal:

> I'm speechless, in awe—words fail me.
> I should never have opened my mouth!
> I've talked too much, way too much.
> I'm ready to shut up and listen.

> JOB 40:3-5, *THE MESSAGE*

> What situations typically cause you to go completely silent?

Read Proverbs 10:19. How would you synopsize this verse into a five-words-or-less book or movie title?

Read Ephesians 4:29. Who among your friends and family "looks like" this verse?

KEY POINTS TO PONDER IN JOB'S STORY

Although God's speech at the end of Job is often recounted as threatening in its tone, some commentators argue that in focusing on creation—the sky, the ocean, the stars, the animals—God chose a course that was more gentle than authoritative. One of my favorite modern-day scholars on Job, Dr. David Atkinson, put it this way:

> However, it may rather be that there is a gentle irony to the tone, and the questions are not threatening, but rather educative: the sort of questions a good teacher may ask a child in order to elicit understanding. It is as though the Lord God is taking a walk through his creation—a walk through the Garden, perhaps, as the storm becomes still—and is inviting Job to accompany him: Do you see this … ? Do you recognize that … ? As Jesus later invited his disciples to "consider the lilies," so here God is inviting Job to consider the beauty and order and wonder of the created world.[1]

Another interesting observation of God's speech is that with the exception of the horse, all of the other creatures He lists under His purview aren't domesticated—the lion (Job 38:39-40), ravens (38:41), the mountain goats (39:1-4), the wild donkey (39:5-8), the wild ox (39:9-12), the ostrich (39:13-18), the hawk (39:26), and the falcon (39:27-30)—the implication being that they are beyond the control of mankind. This has led some scholars to believe it could be an allegorical list of animals, which would be congruent with how the Wisdom books, such as Proverbs, use similes drawn from nature to elucidate moral principles (Prov. 25:11-14).

And then there's the mysterious monsters God lauds in Job 40–41:

> Look at Behemoth,
> which I made along with you.
> He eats grass like cattle.
> Look at the strength of his back
> and the power in the muscles of his belly.
> He stiffens his tail like a cedar tree;
> the tendons of his thighs are woven firmly together.
> His bones are bronze tubes;
> his limbs are like iron rods.
> He is the foremost of God's works;
> only his Maker can draw the sword against him.
> The hills yield food for him,

while all sorts of wild animals play there.
He lies under the lotus plants,
hiding in the protection of marshy reeds.
Lotus plants cover him with their shade;
the willows by the brook surround him.
Though the river rages, Behemoth is unafraid;
he remains confident, even if the Jordan surges up to his mouth.
Can anyone capture him while he looks on,
or pierce his nose with snares?
JOB 40:15-24

Can you pull in Leviathan with a hook
or tie his tongue down with a rope?
Can you put a cord through his nose
or pierce his jaw with a hook?
Will he beg you for mercy
or speak softly to you?
Will he make a covenant with you
so that you can take him as a slave forever?
Can you play with him like a bird
or put him on a leash for your girls?
Will traders bargain for him
or divide him among the merchants?
Can you fill his hide with harpoons
or his head with fishing spears?
Lay a hand on him.
You will remember the battle
and never repeat it!
Any hope of capturing him proves false.
Does a person not collapse at the very sight of him?
No one is ferocious enough to rouse Leviathan;
who then can stand against me?
Who confronted me, that I should repay him?
Everything under heaven belongs to me.
JOB 41:1-11

There's no theological consensus concerning whether Behemoth, which God describes as the fiercest land animal, and Leviathan, which God describes as the fiercest sea animal, are real creatures or mythological. Based on the detailed descriptions of each, many have argued that Behemoth (the plural form of the Hebrew word for "beast") is a hippopotamus and that Leviathan is either a giant crocodile or some kind of whale. But no one knows for sure.[2] What we can glean from the fantastical nature of these magnificently terrifying creatures is that God is greater still! Dr. Francis Andersen put it this way:

> If even the most courageous man would not be so insane
> as to *stir up* Leviathan, how could anyone be so foolhardy
> as to *stand up* against God, as Job has done?[3]

What animal is the most awe-inspiring to you? Explain.

Read Revelation 4:6-8. Do you think these creatures were literal or symbolic? Why do you think Scripture, all of which is breathed by God (2 Tim. 3:16-17), includes such fantastical creatures?

Read Job 41:10-11. Does this part of God's speech make you feel more safe or intimidated? Do you think awe is a necessary component of obeisance/absolute submission? Why or why not?

KEY CHARACTER IN JOB'S STORY

The key character in Job's story—in all of our stories—is God. The One who spoke the world as we know it—and the millions of galaxies we don't even have the capacity to know—into existence. The One who commands the sun when to rise and set. The One who tells the ocean, "You can only come this far." The One who is and is to come. Of course, the Alpha and Omega isn't actually a "key character" in anyone's story. He is the story. Apart from His narrative, we wouldn't exist, much less have any meaning. As an ancient poet wrote about Zeus but Paul correctly ascribed to God:

> For in him we live and move and have our being, as even some of your own poets have said, "For we are also his offspring."
> ACTS 17:28

Yet, just like Job, all too often we forget His supremacy and are deluded into thinking that we are the authors of our own stories—the wind beneath our own fragile wings.

Blaise Pascal was a renowned seventeenth century French mathematician, inventor, and theologian who famously said, "God made man in his own image and man returned the compliment."[4] The clear takeaway of the last few chapters of Job is that we need to reimagine ourselves as characters in God's story, utterly dependent on and submissive to His plotline, which will definitely conclude in a way that is absolutely for our good and His glory—even if some antagonist seems to be hijacking our happy ending in the middle of the story!

> When you review your life, what are two or three chapters in your story that you wish God had written differently? Explain your answer.

What's the first thought that comes to your mind after reading the following Abraham Kuyper quote: "There is not a square inch in the whole domain of our human existence over which Christ, who is Sovereign over *all*, does not cry, '*Mine!*'"[5]?

Read Psalm 8:3-4. How would you paraphrase this so that a child could understand it?

YOUR STORY

Carve out at least an hour to be completely alone with God, preferably in an outdoor setting where you can appreciate His creation. Bring a notebook and your Bible. At the beginning of the hour, read both John 10:27 and Job 40:3-5 out loud. Then open your notebook or journal, and ask God to speak to you. Write down whatever you sense Him saying.

SHOWING LOVE TO GRIEVING FRIENDS

BY HEATHER WARFIELD

Almost exactly a year ago, unspeakable tragedy rocked the world of one of my closest friends. As I sat in a memorial service on a sunny Sunday afternoon, I remember looking toward my friend and her grieving family and thinking, helplessly and hopelessly, "What now?" As I've walked with my sweet friend (and, at times, watched her walk alone) through the last twelve months, I've learned that grief takes many forms, depending on the person and situation and day and hour and moment. There is no cure-all or Band-Aid® or *Grief for Dummies* workbook. But there are a few consistent truths about grief that can help you show hospitality to those you know walking through the process.

1. KNOW YOUR PLACE AND ROLE.

To walk alongside a grieving friend is a privilege. Grief is a sacred place, and if your friend is willing to let you into her pain, consider it an honor and treat it as such. However, on the opposite end of the spectrum are lots of people who may be left out of the grieving process. Sometimes, no matter how much you care, your grieving friend might not have place in her heart to let everyone in.

You may desperately want to be there for your friend, but sometimes the best thing you can do is love from a distance and give your friend space. You can ensure she knows you're available for anything she needs, but if the answer is "no" or "not right now," that's OK.

If you find yourself suddenly distanced from a friend you once held dear, remember:

2. GRIEF BELONGS TO THE GRIEVER.

Perhaps the most obvious yet most difficult truth of coming alongside grieving friends is this: it is not about you. I once heard somebody say this and thought, "Of course not! Why would anyone think it was? How selfish!" And then, a month after that sunny Sunday last September, I found myself sitting on my couch sobbing, feeling personally attacked by my grieving friend's silence.

It was then that the words came back to me, and I was forced to come face-to-face with my selfishness.

What was happening was this: I looked at the situation from my limited outside perspective and thought, "If this were me, I'd want _____ ." So I took that assumption, slapped my imaginary feelings on my friend's very real situation, and couldn't understand why I wasn't helping. I didn't take time to understand what she really needed. I once asked, "What can I do to help you?" to which she responded with a shrug, "There is nothing you can do." The biggest mistake I made was not believing her. Your friend's needs might be different. My friend needed space. But because grief belongs to the griever, everyone grieves differently. No matter how well you think you know a person, asking, "What can I do to help you?" is always the best policy.

Please also note that this question is different from the commonly expressed sentiment, "I'm here if you need anything." Asking a question that makes the griever assess her needs, something she might not be actively doing in her upside-down state of mind.

And the best response to the question? Respect the answer. Then …

3. FOLLOW UP.

While being careful not to bombard, following up is of utmost importance. After the relatives leave and routines return to normal, your friend is still trying to navigate through the surreal, fog-like state that is day-to-day life in the wake of grief. Once the dust has settled, it's another good time to ask, "What can I do to help you?" But, again, respect whatever her answer may be.

If she wants to be alone, offer to babysit so she can get out of the house. If she says she's overwhelmed with daily life, ask if you can run errands, clean her house, or pay bills. If she wants to be distracted, watch a funny movie together. And if she wants to talk, remember:

4. LISTEN MORE THAN YOU SPEAK.

If your friend does invite you into the sacred space of her grief, always listen more than you speak. This is a good rule for life in general, but especially in grief. Even if you've been through something similar, remember #2 and refrain from placing your emotions on her situation. And even though they're tempting and seem like they might be helpful, avoid clichés.

Clichés include, but aren't limited to:
This was God's will.
At least you have other children.
Be thankful he didn't suffer.
Time heals all wounds.

While there is truth behind each of these statements and the griever likely understands the sentiment you're trying to convey, these words simply aren't helpful. Rather than respecting the grieving process, statements like these ignore legitimate emotions and attempt to replace them with happy thoughts.

As author and researcher Brené Brown points out, "Rarely can a response make something better. What makes something better is connection."[6] Margaret Feinberg suggests this connection can be made by saying "seven magic words": I'm thinking of you and praying for you. And then, with everything you have …[7]

5. PRAY.

Be a prayer warrior for your friend. No matter how much you are able to help your friend through a difficult time, God is the Healer and binder of wounds. He draws near to the brokenhearted in ways we'll never be able to. He is the Creator and lover of souls. Practical help, listening empathetically, and respecting needs are all important and should not be disregarded, but prayer will change hearts in ways that our actions can't. Because hallelujah, we have a God who hears, listens, and responds.

What about you? Do you have any hints for showing hospitality to grieving friends? In a time of grief, have you experienced hospitality in a profound way?

Adapted from Heather Warfield, "Hospitality Hints: Showing Love to Grieving Friends," *LifeWay Women Blog*, September 10, 2015, accessed on April 11, 2018.

Video sessions available for purchase
or rent at www.LifeWay.com/Job

DISCUSSION QUESTIONS:

What one thing from the video teaching was new or interesting to you?

In what season of life have you seen God the clearest?

When have you seen God bring sweet reconciliation to a personal relationship or to someone close to you? How did God show up in this situation?

When have you experienced unlikely joy in the most trying of circumstances?

Lisa says that we are not to just be consumers of unlikely joy, but carriers of it. How are you accomplishing that in your life?

What are some truths that have really stood out for you in this study of Job?

How has God changed your heart about the way you view pain and the way you view Him in your suffering?

7

YOUR
JOURNAL OF
UNLIKELY JOY

READING ASSIGNMENT:

At some point between now and putting this hopefully dog-eared and coffee-stained study guide on a shelf, please peruse Job 42:7-17. Read through the passage at least twice so that the meaning behind these words really sinks in.

MY STORY

Every Christmas Day, sometime after the festive presents have been opened and the sumptuous meal has been consumed, my heart swells with an emotion that lies somewhere between contentment and wistful. That's what I'm feeling right now. Perusing Job's story for more than a year now has taught me how to better rest in God's sovereign goodness regardless of what's going on in my little corner of the world. Job's well-lived life has helped soften some of my sharpest edges in a spiritual Velveteen Rabbit kind of way. Even though I'm partly convinced that the medley of first-world problems we experienced this past year—our ongoing bug-tastrophe, the demise of our HVAC and plumbing systems, giant rocks falling off our chimney and crashing to the ground right behind me, major car repairs, three surgeries, and me almost losing a pointer finger in Australia—were somehow the empathetic price-of-admission I had to pay for choosing to teach on Job, I'm really going to miss this guy! The path he navigated through pain became a wise course to follow, helping me stand firm in my seasons of distress. But it also became a sort of treasure map leading to unlikely joy.

And the proverbial pot of gold at the end of Job's rainbow is filled with God's blessings:

> After Job had prayed for his friends, *the* LORD *restored his fortunes and doubled his previous possessions.* All his brothers, sisters, and former acquaintances came to him and dined with him in his house. They sympathized with him and comforted him concerning all the adversity the LORD had brought on him. Each one gave him a piece of silver and a gold earring.
>
> So the LORD blessed the last part of Job's life more than the first. He owned fourteen thousand sheep and goats, six thousand camels, one thousand yoke of oxen, and one thousand female donkeys. He also had seven sons and three daughters. He named his first daughter Jemimah, his second Keziah, and his third Keren-happuch. *No women as beautiful as Job's daughters could be found in all the land, and their father granted them an inheritance with their brothers.*
>
> *Job lived 140 years after this and saw his children and their children to the fourth generation.* Then Job died, old and full of days.
>
> JOB 42:10-17, *EMPHASIS MINE*

First, the number of livestock God grants Job here in the finale is exactly double the number that were taken in Job 1:3, which may be our Redeemer's wry nod to the law of Exodus 22:4, a mandate that a thief—when caught—must repay double of what he stole. Obviously, God is not a thief, nor can He steal what He already owns. And He's the Supreme Cowboy who owns the cattle on a thousand hills (Ps. 50:10). The fact is God purposefully doubles what was taken from Job, as well as doubles his lifespan (Job 42:16). Seventy years was the normal male life span according to Psalm 90:10; therefore, Job's one hundred and forty year life span was twice what was considered normal in this era. This may very well be our Lord's way of speaking to Job's continual complaint that he was unjustly "robbed" of his livelihood, loved ones, and good name. In light of the significance of numerology in this Biblical era, this overt two-fold compensation in chapter 42 provides, at the very least, tacit redemption of Job's reputation.[1]

The second thing that made my heart do a happy dance is that not only are Job's three daughters named here—which is unlikely in the Hebrew Bible as female names were considered "profane" because they were taken from everyday objects instead of encapsulating a prayer or theological truism like most male names[2]—but they're also described in Cinderella-like terms, as being the most beautiful in all the land. Then, to top it off, Job gives his gorgeous girls an inheritance like their brothers, which in their ancient culture was as wildly unlikely as finding a hot dog vendor at a vegan festival would be in ours! The unlikely mention of women being valued in this very misogynistic time period is yet another divine affirmation that the first shall be last and the last shall be first (Matt. 20:16). It also reminds us that our heavenly Father is especially tender toward His children who've been missed or marginalized. If you feel like you've been overlooked in your season of grief, I pray you're deeply comforted by the favorable treatment of Job's daughters, which serves as tangible proof that nothing in your life is hidden from God. He will ultimately turn your mourning into dancing (Ps. 30:11).

> In light of the unlikely favor Job's daughter's received, how have you felt affirmed through the promises of this true Old Testament story?

Now, to finish this journey, we're going to chunk the study format we've been using and adopt a less formal, review kind of style to kick off the after-party. So grab a happy-colored marker—like hot pink or turquoise—and let's start dancing down memory lane!

FROM THE SESSION 1 TEACHING VIDEO

While the idea of deservedness may seem logical, it isn't biblical. In fact, turn with me to Matthew 5:43-45:

> You have heard that it was said, Love your neighbor and hate your enemy. But I tell you, love your enemies and pray for those who persecute you, so that you may be children of your Father in heaven. For he causes his sun to rise on the evil and the good, and sends rain on the righteous and the unrighteous.
>
> MATTHEW 5:43-45

Here at the tail end of His Sermon on the Mount, Jesus blows the idea of deservedness right out of the water. Now let's head to the right, to Luke 13:1-5:

> At that time, some people came and reported to him about the Galileans whose blood Pilate had mixed with their sacrifices. And he responded

to them, "Do you think that these Galileans were more sinful than all the other Galileans because they suffered these things? No, I tell you; but unless you repent, you will all perish as well. Or those eighteen that the tower in Siloam fell on and killed—do you think they were more sinful than all the other people who live in Jerusalem? No, I tell you; but unless you repent, you will all perish as well."

LUKE 13:1-5

This passage is regarded as one of the "hard sayings" of Jesus because it's difficult to swallow. He once again dispels the myth of deservedness by essentially saying what humanity truly deserves is death.

Yikers. That'll blow your hard drive, won't it? That means, no matter how many Bible study blanks we've filled in, how often we volunteer at Vacation Bible School, or how many meals we've served to the homeless, we can't earn one of those immunity sticks like they do on the reality show *Survivor*. None of us can be good enough to shield ourselves and those we love from suffering. Job proves that good people—including people of faith—can and do experience horrific things according to the permissive will of God. And this by no particular fault of their own. Job's faith did not prevent his agony; it actually produced it.

Now before you chunk this Bible study into the trash, let's make the turn toward home with some unlikely good news:

God wasn't punishing Job; He was promoting him. I mean, just reread Job 1:8:

> Then the LORD said to Satan, "Have you considered my servant Job? No one else on earth is like him, a man of perfect integrity, who fears God and turns away from evil."

It was like God was saying, *Have you considered my main man Job, you slithery liar? He is faithful. He won't turn away from me no matter how high you turn up the heat on him!* It almost seems like the Creator of the universe has taken up the role of Job's publicist. God doesn't remove His hand of protection as some have taught. Instead God holds Job up before Satan and launches into a sales pitch. In the economy of God, Job's suffering was not a *demotion*, it was a *promotion*. An honor. A privilege. The Lord quite literally picked Job for the honorable position of carrying the weight of pain in much the same way the host country of each Olympics picks the final torchbearer to light the Olympic flame in the opening ceremonies. God chose Job with the foreknowledge that he would submit to carry suffering well.

Can you imagine how different our lives could be if we began to view pain as a divine—albeit unlikely—privilege? If we could see our suffering as a difficult journey God handpicked us to embark on because He knows we're strong enough to make the trek and knows His glory will be illuminated through our efforts? Changing our perspective on suffering—viewing it as an honor instead of dumb luck or degrading—could absolutely change the course of our lives and deeply impact the world around us.

> What was your initial reaction to the revelation in Session 1 that God wasn't punishing Job but rather was promoting him through his season of suffering and loss?

> How has that unique vantage point on pain changed the way you view some of the hardships/heartbreaks in your life?

FROM THE SESSION 2 VIDEO TEACHING

Stoicism is not a spiritual gift, y'all!

Job emotes greatly and laments loudly in Job 3 and is still within the bounds of completely appropriate behavior for a believer. Because how we grieve isn't what gets us in trouble; it's what we grieve that can crack the door open for sin to creep in. Job was so understandably devastated that he cursed the day he was born, but he didn't curse God. As a matter of fact, based on the Hebraic style of his poetic speech, he was praying to God.

While doing research for this Bible study I read an article that compared Job to Jean-Paul Sartre, the infamous French existentialist who was well-known for his communistic ideology, despair, and atheism. One of Sartre's most memorable quotes is: "Every existing thing is born without reason, prolongs itself out of weakness, and dies by chance."[3] If you took a philosophy course in college, you probably remember that woven into most of Sartre's published works is the theme that there is no God and therefore no divine meaning or purpose to our lives. Yet his adamant unbelief was the source of his torment because Sartre also said: "That God does not exist, I cannot deny. That my whole being cries out for God I cannot forget."[4]

We need to understand there's a colossal difference between disagreeing with God and denying His existence altogether. Job cursed the day he was born and expressed confusion, frustration, and even anger at God over allowing such tragedies to befall him, but he did not reject God. In fact, the tormented exasperation Job hurls toward God proves that he is anything but an atheist.

I dated a wrestler in high school and college who taught me that no matter how difficult your match was, you should never give up and go limp because that's when you were most likely to get pinned by your opponent. Even if we're on our spiritual backs, we have to keep arching in faith. And be encouraged, because not only is our faith a gift from God, it's more resilient than Gumby®—it will stretch far beyond what you think is your capacity to endure. Anguish doesn't distance us from God, giving up does.

> What was your initial reaction to Job's anguished honest wish that he could die (Job 7)?

> How did the way Job processed his pain affect the way you will process personal pain and grief in the future?

FROM THE SESSION 3 VIDEO TEACHING

The silver lining in Job's dark cloud that enabled him to profess hope in God no matter what is found in Job 14:14-15:

> When a person dies, will he come back to life?
> If so, I would wait all the days of my struggle

until my relief comes.
You would call, and I would answer you.
You would long for the work of your hands.

OK, now get this, Job was probably written somewhere between one thousand and fifteen hundred years before the birth of Jesus Christ. That means Job existed long before the idea of resurrection became part of Jewish consciousness. According to the prevailing logic of this ancient era of redemptive history, the concept of resurrection was no doubt as alien to Job as rockets or cell phones. And yet here he is clearly expressing his belief that even if he died God could restore him. Then he raises the bar even higher by insisting that God would *long* to restore him. I think pain and suffering make the veil between our world and glory thinner. I think heartbreak helps us see divine things we're oblivious to otherwise. I think the fruit of crystal clear spiritual vision only grows in the soil of sorrow.

That word *long* in our English Bibles is translated from the Hebrew word *kacaph,* and it literally means *to pine for, yearn for, or desire strongly.* In Greek, the word is *epipotheō* (eh-pip-ah-they-oh), and Paul uses it at the beginning of his Letter to the Romans when he writes: I want *very much* to see you (Rom. 1:11). In other biblical passages, the word *long* has a decidedly romantic undertone. In all the muck and misery of Job's experience, there's this one gleaming diamond that keeps him from falling apart—the audacious hope that God loves him so much that even if he dies God will restore him! Job was pointing forward to the work of Christ on the cross.

> He is the image of the invisible God, the firstborn over all creation. For everything was created by him, in heaven and on earth, the visible and the invisible, whether thrones or dominions or rulers or authorities—all things have been created through him and for him. He is before all things, and by him all things hold together.
>
> COLOSSIANS 1:15-17

The hope of what Jesus would accomplish on that old rugged cross is what held Job together during what is arguably one of the most painful personal experiences in human history. And what Jesus accomplished on the cross for us—redemption from the fall and restoration into a right relationship with our heavenly Father—is what will hold you and I together during the painful seasons of our lives too.

What was your initial reaction to Job's Messianic references?

How has God made the veil "thinner" for you through this Bible study?

FROM THE SESSION 4 VIDEO TEACHING

We were created to be heard by God; instead we settle for a few likes on Facebook®.

We were created to be held by God; instead we settle for a few pats on the back or the kiss of an enemy.

We were created to be healed by God; instead we settle by medicating ourselves with alcohol or narcotics or carbohydrates or reality television or shopping.

The false sense of community with people we've never even met on social media is vaccinating us to what we need most, which is real intimacy with the only real God.

Job's honesty about desperately needing intimacy is what drives him to a triumphant epiphany at the lowest point of his tragic circumstances, where he finds unlikely joy at the very end of his proverbial rope.

> But I know that my Redeemer lives,
> and at the end he will stand on the dust.
> Even after my skin has been destroyed,
> yet I will see God in my flesh.
> I will see him myself;
> my eyes will look at him, and not as a stranger.
> My heart longs within me.

JOB 19:25-27

The Hebrew word Job uses here for *Redeemer* is *ga'al* (pronounced go-ale). Elsewhere in Scripture *ga'al* is used to describe a kinsman redeemer, which was usually a close relative who stepped in to rescue someone in their covenant family who was in trouble. It could mean rescuing someone from a relatively mild emergency by paying off a debt, intervening in a major emergency by redeeming them from being sold into slavery, or in the case of a marital emergency, a kinsman redeemer could step in and marry a widow, thereby rescuing her from an impoverished existence and the shame of being childless by giving her a son, as Boaz did for Ruth. A kinsman redeemer could also serve as an advocate in the case of a legal emergency, formally taking up the cause and case of a relative that had gotten into trouble.

What makes Job's use of *ga'al* especially interesting is that in Job 16:9, he called God his adversary. So this passage indicates Job needs a Redeemer to take up his cause with his Redeemer. A *ga'al* to stand in the gap between him and *ga'al* God. It almost sounds like the spiritual version of "Who's on first" doesn't it? It'd be like me saying *I need you to be my hero and protect me from you, who's been bullying me!* It's crazy talk, unless you look down the time line of redemptive history to Jesus and realize that He is the Kinsman Redeemer who adjudicated our guilty verdict of sin before God the Father by taking our death penalty upon Himself. God the Redeemer wore the black robe of divine Judge, and Jesus the Redeemer shrugged into an orange jumpsuit originally meant for us. Only a perfectly compassionate God would make Himself *ga'al* squared so that we could be heard, held, healed, and saved from never-ending sorrow and torment.

This pivotal chapter in Job's story is a powerful reminder that the sweetest miracles often grow in the hardest soil and that divine joy often crashes the pity party when we least expect it.

When, recently, have you been able to relate to Job's need to be heard and held?

What is the most beautiful bloom you've seen in your life in the middle of a kind of winter season?

FROM THE SESSION 5 VIDEO TEACHING

After months and months of study, I'm still not sure whether to put Elihu in a white hat or a black hat. But I have decided that despite his questionable methodology, some of his message is spot on—especially in how he insists that when God allows us to suffer it is not punitive.

> For God speaks time and again,
> but a person may not notice it.
> In a dream, a vision in the night,
> when deep sleep comes over people
> as they slumber on their beds,
> *he uncovers their ears*
> *and terrifies them with warnings,*
> in order to turn a person from his actions
> and suppress the pride of a person.
> God spares his soul from the Pit,
> his life from crossing the river of death.
> A person may be disciplined on his bed with pain
> and constant distress in his bones,
> so that he detests bread,
> and his soul despises his favorite food.
> His flesh wastes away to nothing,
> and his unseen bones stick out.
> He draws near to the Pit,

and his life to the executioners.
If there is an angel on his side,
one mediator out of a thousand,
to tell a person what is right for him
and to be gracious to him and say,

"Spare him from going down to the Pit;
I have found a ransom,"
then his flesh will be healthier than in his youth,
and he will return to the days of his youthful vigor.

JOB 33:14-25, *EMPHASIS MINE*

I love the imagery of verse 16—God uncovers our ears with pain. In other words, He gets our attention with hardship. You've probably heard the old adage that when you're flat on your back, you're forced to look up. Or when you get to the end of yourself, you get to the beginning of God. While these sayings may sound like simple platitudes, they're actually rooted in redemptive narrative.

It wasn't until Abraham was holding a knife over his own son's neck that he recognized God's merciful provision. It wasn't until Moses was exiled on the back side of the desert that God called him into full-time ministry. It wasn't until Jonah was neck deep in whale bile that he became obedient to God's will. It wasn't until Peter threw Jesus under a (figurative) bus that he was restored and became the rock of the early church. It wasn't until Paul was flat on his back frantically rubbing his eyes on the shoulder of the Damascus Freeway that he encountered the living Messiah. When everything falls apart, God gets our full attention!

And while all pain isn't divinely causative—God doesn't cause evil like human trafficking or disease like cancer—all pain does have a divine purpose.

When I was 11 years old my uncle accidentally ran me over. He was staying with us because he became an alcoholic after fighting in the Korean War, which led to the loss of his family and eventually homelessness. So my dad brought him to live with us in the hopes of helping him dry out. But my sweet uncle just couldn't make it through the day without medicating with booze. And one Valentine's Day when I was in the sixth grade, he and my dad were arguing over the fact that he was drunk yet again in the middle of the afternoon. In anger, he drove off in his Buick®. He didn't see me bending down to pick up a Frisbee® behind his car so he backed over me, then he put the car in drive to speed away from my yelling father, not realizing dad was running toward him screaming and waving his hands because I was underneath his car.

My back was fractured in five places that day, and I've had two major surgeries since—one on my lower back and one to put a titanium plate in my neck to fuse C4, 5, and 6 together. As one physician put it, "That accident drained the bank account of your back, honey, and any check you write on it now is gonna bounce." However, the pain of two complete discectomies, having my throat cut, and six screws drilled into my neck vertebrae to fasten a titanium plate on the front of my neck was totally different than the pain of the car accident. The accident caused a rupturing kind of pain, while the pain of the surgeries was rehabilitative. One tore me apart, while the other put me back together.

The pain that sifts through our Redeemer's hands is not punitive because Jesus took all the punishment we deserved on the cross. Therefore the idea that bad things have happened to us because God is punishing us is not theologically sound. However, suffering can be a very rehabilitative means of grace as the psalmist attests to in Psalm 119:

> I know, LORD, that your judgments are just
> and that you have afflicted me fairly.
>
> PSALM 119:75

We may feel like we're being torn apart, but in actuality, we're being torn away from whatever was pulling us apart from God. Which means that the ultimate end of suffering is spiritual healing and wholeness.

> What did God "say" to you the last time He uncovered your ears through hardship?

When have you experienced rehabilitative pain?

FROM THE SESSION 6 VIDEO TEACHING

I trust you've come to the understanding that pain and suffering are a universal aspect of the human condition. Just like death and taxes, we will all experience hardship at some level. And after marinating in Job's story for more than a year now, I've come to believe that whether hardship makes us bitter or better depends on how we respond to it—whether we primarily seek answers that will somehow explain the reason for our pain or whether we find more comfort in God's presence than in trying to figure it all out.

The comfort we are so desperate for, especially in times of suffering, is not found in answers. It's found in the abiding presence of God. Whether we recognize it or not, what our souls long for most isn't a logical explanation for our pain but for a divine companion in the midst of it.

In the middle of the almost maddening grief that followed the death of his beloved wife, Joy, C. S. Lewis put it like this in his classic book *A Grief Observed*:

> If I knew that to be eternally divided from H. [his pet name for his wife] and eternally forgotten by her would add a greater joy and splendour to her being, of course I'd say, "Fire ahead." Just as if, on earth, I could have cured her cancer by never seeing her again, I'd have arranged never to see her again. I'd have had to. Any decent person would. But that's quite different. That's not the situation I'm in.
>
> When I lay these questions before God I get no answer. But a rather special sort of "No answer." It is not the locked door. It is more like a silent, certainly not uncompassionate, gaze. As though He shook His head not in refusal but waiving the question. Like, "Peace, child; you don't understand."[5]

Peace, child, you don't understand could very well be the poignant title of the last four chapters of Job. And if we can learn to quiet our souls in the face of God's sometimes inscrutable kindness as Sir Lewis and Job did, it's also the gateway to unlikely joy.

What questions are less urgent for you to have answered as a result of studying Job?

How has one of your "Why did this happen to me?" questions been silenced by a "Who is God to me?" answer?

What would you describe as the biggest spiritual jewel you discovered on this journey we've taken through Job?

LEADER HELPS

SESSION 1

1. Greet and welcome participants to the study of *Job: A Story of Unlikely Joy*. Use the following questions to get some discussion rolling with your group:

   - What drew you to this study of Job?
   - Before we dive in, what are some things you already know about Job?
   - How are you approaching this study? With a little fear? Excitement? Explain.
   - What do you most hope to gain from this Bible study? Discuss a few goals you hope to accomplish through this study.

2. Play the Session 1 video teaching.

3. Following the video, use the questions on page 9 to review the video teaching.

4. Close by giving the women in your group the opportunity to share deep hurts or difficulties they or those close to them are walking through. Spend time praying for these needs.

SESSION 2

1. Welcome participants back to *Job: A Story of Unlikely Joy*. Use the following questions to prompt discussion about last week's personal study:

   - What was the most significant thing you learned from your personal study this week?
   - Do you tend to run toward people in pain to offer your help, or do you hope someone else will step in to nurse their wounds? Explain.
   - How do you feel about God allowing Satan to afflict Job?
   - How has a painful experience in your life turned into a blessing? *moving to CA*

   - How has that experienced shaped your view of God?

2. Play the Session 2 video teaching.

3. Following the video, use the questions on page 35 to review the video teaching.

4. Close by leading women to form groups of three or four. Provide time for them to pray for each other. Check on those who shared deep hurts last week, and continue to pray for them.

SESSION 3

1. Welcome participants back to *Job: A Story of Unlikely Joy*. Use the following questions to prompt discussion about last week's personal study:

   - What was the most significant thing you learned from your personal study this week?
   - When was a time your pain and despair isolated you from others?
   - Have you ever had someone speak truth to you but do so in the wrong spirit? What effect did it have on you? Have you ever been guilty of speaking truth without love? Explain.
   - Is it OK to question God? Explain.
   - Why is a friend's *presence* sometimes more comforting than her *words*?

2. Play the Session 3 video teaching.

3. Following the video, use the questions on page 59 to review the video teaching.

4. Close the study by giving women time to consider the kind of comforters they have been to those around them who are hurting. Provide time for personal prayers of repentance and commitment,

asking God to make us all more compassionate comforters.

SESSION 4

1. Welcome participants back to *Job: A Story of Unlikely Joy*. Use the following questions to prompt discussion about last week's personal study:

   - What was the most significant thing you learned from your personal study this week? ~~78+79~~
   - Have you ever adopted a "fake it till you make it" attitude to survive a difficult season? Explain. *back pain*
   - Why do we sometimes struggle to be authentic? Are there specific relationships or situations where it feels almost impossible to be real? Explain.
   - How do you feel about Jesus knowing every single thing about you? Does that comfort you? Scare you? Or something else?
   - Do you feel the freedom to fully and honestly express your heart to God? Why or why not?

2. Play the Session 4 video teaching.

3. Following the video, use the questions on page 81 to review the video teaching.

4. Close with a time of worship. This could be as extensive as enlisting someone to lead you in worship songs or as simple as reading a few psalms together, or both.

SESSION 5

1. Welcome participants back to *Job: A Story of Unlikely Joy*. Use the following questions to prompt discussion about last week's personal study:

   - What was the most significant thing you learned from your personal study this week?
   - How have you seen a recent problem turn into a praise?
   - This week, did you have more rainy days or sunny ones? Explain.
   - In your darkest times, how have you seen God's light break through?
   - Is it possible to be woeful and worshipful at the same time? Explain. When have you experienced this?
   - How are you continually seeing God work through the relationships, situations, and circumstances with which you're struggling?

2. Play the Session 5 video teaching.

3. Following the video, use the questions on page 105 to review the video teaching.

4. Close the session by directing the women to form groups of three or four. Lead them to discuss how God has used difficult seasons in their lives to grow them. After sharing together, encourage them to pray for one another.

SESSION 6

1. Welcome participants back to *Job: A Story of Unlikely Joy*. Use the following questions to prompt discussion about last week's personal study:

   - What was the most significant thing you learned from your personal study this week?
   - How have you seen unresolved pain from someone's past negatively affect his or her present life? Has this been the case for you? Explain.

- Why is consistent repentance so necessary for our spiritual lives?
- Is feeling shame and being repentant the same thing? Explain.
- Why is it difficult to have a teachable heart during a time of pain? Why is it necessary?
- Who has God used to pave the way for spiritual renewal in your life?

2. Play the Session 6 video teaching.

3. Following the video, use the questions on page 129 to review the video teaching.

4. Close by leading your group in prayer, asking God to open your hearts to hear Him. Thank Him for being a God who hears and a God who speaks.

SESSION 7

1. Welcome participants back to *Job: A Story of Unlikely Joy*. Use the following questions to prompt discussion about last week's personal study:

- What was the most significant thing you learned from your personal study this week?
- What's a personal example of a "rupture to rapture" season?
- Have you ever found yourself in a situation before God when you realized you may have talked too much and just needed to be silent? Explain.
- Share an awe-inspiring moment you have experienced with God.
- When you review your life, what are two or three chapters in your story you wish God had written differently? Explain.

2. Play the Session 7 video teaching.

3. Following the video, use the questions on page 153 to review the video teaching.

4. Close the session by giving women the opportunity to share their greatest takeaway from this study. Then spend a few moments allowing those you've been praying for to express how God has ministered to them.

ENDNOTES

WEEK 1

1. Philip D. Yancey, *Where Is God When It Hurts?* (Grand Rapids, MI: Zondervan, 1977).
2. D. A. Carson, Richard Phillips (ed.), *Only One Way?* (Wheaton, IL: Crossway Books, 2006), 134.
3. Allen C. Myers (ed.), *The Eerdmans Bible Dictionary* (Grand Rapids, MI: William B. Eerdmans Publishing Company, 1987), 1032.
4. David J. A. Clines, *Word Biblical Commentary: Job 1–20* (Grand Rapids, MI: Zondervan, 1989), lx, accessed via MyWsb.com on March 21, 2018.
5. David S. Dockery (ed.), *Holman Concise Bible Commentary* (Nashville: B&H Publishing Group, 1998), 202-203, accessed on March 26, 2018 via MyWsb.com.
6. Ibid, Clines, lvii.
7. Francis I. Andersen, *Tyndale Old Testament Commentaries: Job* (Downers Grove, IL: InterVarsity Press, 1976), 75.
8. David J. Atkinson, *The Bible Speaks Today: The Message of Job* (Downer's Grove, IL: InterVarsity Press, 1991), 16.
9. Ibid, Andersen, 21.
10. Ibid, Atkinson, 23.
11. Ibid.
12. Ibid, Andersen, 97.
13. D. Stuart Briscoe, *The Preacher's Commentary Series, Volumes 1-35* (Nashville: Thomas Nelson, 2010.)
14. C. S. Lewis, *The Chronicles of Narnia: The Lion, The Witch and the Wardrobe* (New York City: HarperCollins Publishers, 1950), 146.
15. See Lindsay Wilson, "Job" in *Theological Interpretation of the Old Testament*, gen. ed. Kevin J. Vanhoozer (Grand Rapids: Baker Academic, 2008), 148.
16. See Joel S. Allen, "Job 3: History of Interpretation" in *Dictionary of the Old Testament: Wisdom, Poetry and Writings* [DWPW], ed. Tremper Longman III and Peter Enns (Downers Grove, IL: IVP Academic, 2008), 366.
17. H. H. Rowley, *Job* (London: Marshall, Morgan & Scott, 1976), 20.
18. See Stephen G. Dempster, *Dominion and Dynasty: A Biblical Theology of the Hebrew Bible* (Downers Grove, IL: InterVarsity Press, 2003), 202.
19. See John H. Walton, "Job 1: Book of" in *DWPW*, 340-41.
20. Ibid., 337-38.
21. Dempster, *Dominion and Dynasty*, 203.

WEEK 2

1. Ella Wheeler Wilcox, *Poems of Passion* (Chicago: Belford, Clarke & Co., Publishers, 1883), 131-132.
2. Ibid.
3. A. W. Tozer, *Delighting In God* (Bloomington, MN: Bethany House, 2015), 11.

4. Dwight Lyman Moody (ed. Rev. J. B. McClure), *D. L. Moody's Child Stories Related By Him in His Revival Work in Europe and America, with Pictorial Illustrations* (Chicago: Rhodes & McClure, 1877), 81.
5. Francis I. Andersen, *Job: An Introduction and Commentary*, Tyndale Old Testament Commentary (Downers Grove, Il: InterVarsity Press, 1977), 95.
6. John E. Hartley, *The Book of Job, New International Commentary* (Grand Rapids: William B. Eerdman's Publishing Co., 1988), 86.
7. H. L. Ellison, "Eliphaz" in *International Standard Bible Encyclopedia (ISBE)*, Geoffrey W. Bromiley, gen. ed., vol. 2 (Grand Rapids: William B. Eerdman's Publishing Co., 1982), 69.
8. Ibid, Hartley.
9. H. L. Ellison, "Bildad" in *ISBE*, vol. 1 (1979), 510.
10. H. L. Ellison, "Zophar" in *ISBE*, vol. 4 (1988), 1210.
11. J. W. Watts, *Old Testament Teaching* (Nashville: Broadman Press, 1967), 134.

WEEK 3

1. Adapted from: Lisa Harper, *The Sacrament of Happy* (Nashville: B&H Publishing Group, 2017), 5-8. Excerpt courtesy of and used by permission of B&H Publishing Group.

2. Duane A. Garrett, *The New American Commentary – Proverbs, Ecclesiastes, and Song of Songs, Volume 14* (Nashville: B&H Publishing Group, 1993), 220.

3. Ibid.

4. Brennan Manning, *Ruthless Trust* (New York: HarperCollins, 2000), 44-45.

5. Ibid.

6. Ibid, 48.

7. Arthur Blessitt Evangelistic Association, *The Official Website of Arthur Blessitt – Homepage*, http://www.blessitt.com/ Accessed on March 29, 2018.

8. Arthur Blessitt Evangelistic Association, *The Official Website of Arthur Blessitt* – Facts and Figures, http://www.blessitt.com/fascinating-facts-and-figures/, Accessed on March 29, 2018.

9. Ibid, *The Official Website of Arthur Blessitt – Homepage*.

WEEK 4

1. Serajul Quadir, "U.N. official says violence and torture continues on Rohingya," *Reuters*.com, March 13, 2018, https://www.reuters.com/article/us-myanmar-rohingya-bangladesh-un/u-n-official-says-violence-and-torture-continues-on-rohingya-idUSKCN1GP26K, accessed on April 2, 2018.

2. Paige Patterson, *The New American Commentary: Revelation, Volume 39* (Nashville: B & H Publishing Group, 2012). Accessed on April 2, 2018 via MyWsb.com.

3. "Strong's H7293," *Blue Letter Bible*, https://www.blueletterbible.org/lang/lexicon/lexicon.cfm?Strongs=H7293&t=CSB, Accessed on April 2, 2018.

4. *The Holman Christian Standard Bible* (Nashville: Holman Bible Publishers, 2010), 878.

5. Michael Card, *A Sacred Sorrow* (Colorado Springs, CO: NavPress, 2005), 7.

6. Ibid.

7. Ibid, 11.

8. John T. McNeill (ed.), *Calvin: Institutes of the Christian Religion* (Louisville, KY: The Westminster John Knox Press, 1960), 121.

9. All Hebrew terms in this article are from Francis Brown, S. R. Driver, and Charles A. Briggs. *The Brown-Driver-Briggs Hebrew and English Lexicon* (Peabody, MA: Hendrickson Publishers, Inc., 2001).

10. Roland DeVaux, *Ancient Israel: Its Life and Institutions* (London: Darton, Longman & Todd, 1961), 157.

WEEK 5

1. C. S. Lewis, *The Problem of Pain* (New York: HarperOne, 1940), 92.

2. William Shakespeare, *Hamlet* (New York: Simon & Schuster Paperbacks, 1992), 151.

3. Robert L. Alden, *The New American Commentary, Job—Vol. 11* (Nashville: Broadman & Holman Publishers, 1993) via MyWsb.com.

4. Four other persons of the same name appear in the Old Testament: (1) a great grandfather of Samuel (1 Sam. 1:1); (2) a leader of the tribe of Manasseh who defected to David (1 Chron. 12:20); (3) a Korahite gatekeeper in the temple (26:7); (4) one of David's brothers, an officer over the tribe of Judah (27:18).

5. Buz is the brother of Uz (Gen. 22:21). Job lived in the land of Uz, thus attaching some possible ancestral Hebraic tie between Job and Elihu. Uz is also the name of a son of Aram, the son of Shem (10:22-23), a further possible linkage. Buz is also mentioned in Jeremiah 25:23 with ties to Teman and Dedan.

6. David L McKenna, *Job, The Communicator's Commentary, Vol. 12* (Waco: Word Books, 1986), 226.

7. Norman C. Habel, *The Book of Job, The Old Testament Library* (Philadelphia: The Westminster Press, 1985), 452.

8. John E. Hartley, *The Book of Job, New International Commentary of the Old Testament* (Grand Rapids: William B. Eerdmans Publishing Company, 1988), 427.

9. Samuel Terrien, *Job: Poet of Existence* (Indianapolis: The Bobbs-Merrill Company, Inc., 1957), 205.

10. Reasons often cited: Elihu not mentioned elsewhere in book; not part of the plot; vocabulary, structure and style are different from the rest of the book. Compare Hartley, 28-30 for evaluation of these positions.

WEEK 6

1. Ibid, Atkinson, 142.

2. Ibid, Andersen, 311-312.

3. Ibid, 312.

4. Blaise Pascal as quoted in Brennan Manning, *Abba's Child* (Colorado Springs, CO: Tyndale, 1994), 3.

5. James D. Bratt, *Abraham Kuyper* (Grand Rapids, MI: Wm. B. Eerdmans Publishing Co., 2013), xx.

6. Brown, Brené. "The Power of Vulnerability." *The RSA.* YouTube Video, 21:47. Posted August 15, 2013. https://www.youtube.com/watch?v=sXSjc-pbXk4.

7. Margaret Feinberg, "The Three Worst Things You Can Say to Someone Battling Cancer or any Kind of Adversity … And You've Probably Already Said Them" *Blog*, October 28, 2013, https://margaretfeinberg.com/three-worst-things-can-say-someone-battling-cancer-kind-adversityand-youve-probably-already-said/, accessed on April 23, 2018.

WEEK 7

1. David J. A. Clines, *Word Biblical Commentary: Job 38–42, Volume 18b* (Nashville: Thomas Nelson: 2011), 1236, accessed via MyWsb.com on May 3, 2018.

2. Ibid, 1237.

3. Jean-Paul Sartre, *Essays in Aesthetics* (New York: Open Road Integrated Media, 2011).

4. Ibid.

5. C. S. Lewis, *A Grief Observed* (New York: HarperOne, 1961), 69.

If You Loved Job, Study with Lisa Harper Live

ABUNDANCE

We went through fire and water, but you brought us out to abundance. Psalm 66:12

A one-day experience where women of all ages and backgrounds come together to celebrate, rest, and find peace in the great abundance of God.

Study with Lisa Harper live
LifeWay.com/Abundance

LifeWay Women | events